A–Z
OF
SOUTHAMPTON
PLACES - PEOPLE - HISTORY

Martin Brisland

AMBERLEY

Acknowledgements

Many people helped in many ways during the writing of this book. My grateful thanks to the Bevois Mount History Group, especially Ken Lymer for the graphic; Greg Gilbert for use of part of his poem; Jenny for all her loving support; Carolina Bastos for her photography and technical assistance; Sotonopaedia online resource; *The Illustrated Guide to Southampton* by Ian Broad (1982); and all my See Southampton tour guide colleagues, especially Sandra.

In loving memory of my parents Alexander Brisland (1921–2002) and Barbara Brisland (1925–99) who always supported me.

First published 2019

Amberley Publishing
The Hill, Stroud, Gloucestershire, GL5 4EP
www.amberley-books.com

Copyright © Martin Brisland, 2019

The right of Martin Brisland to be identified as the Author of this work has been asserted in accordance with the Copyrights, Designs and Patents Act 1988.

ISBN 978 1 4456 8800 8 (print)
ISBN 978 1 4456 8801 5 (ebook)

British Library Cataloguing in Publication Data. A catalogue record for this book is available from the British Library.

Typesetting by Aura Technology and Software Services, India. Printed in Great Britain.

Contents

Introduction

Southampton poet, writer, painter and musician Greg Gilbert wrote of his hometown in the poem 'Holy River':

Where the cranes stitch the horizon,
And the old walls describe the city as was, the shore as was.

Southampton has impressive remains from its time as a walled medieval trading town. Today the Docks are very busy with cruise and container ships. The land reclamation of 1927–34 to create the Western Docks has cut the city centre off from its shoreline. There is public access to Mayflower Park but little else. Southampton can feel a rather disjointed place, defined, along with the Docks, by the rivers Test and Itchen.

There are different centres of activity such as the University of Southampton campus, Bedford Place, the Cultural Quarter, West Quay, Oxford Street and the Old Town. The population can also seem transient with our Southampton and Solent universities, which welcome tens of thousands of students from all over the UK and abroad.

One way to create a sense of belonging and identity is through the use of arts, heritage, culture and sport to create the ties that bind. The 150 entries on people, places, stories and events in this book range from the well known to the more obscure. I hope they make a small contribution to that process and show why I am proud to be a born and bred Sotonian.

Abraham, Edward Penley (1913–99)

Born in Southampton, Edward attended King Edward VI School. He played an important part in the development of the penicillin and cephalosporin antibiotics. There is a blue plaque on his former home in Southview Road, Shirley.

Adam and Eve Statues

These are the popular names given to the two nude statues presented to Southampton by the architects of the post-Second World War Kingsland Housing estate. They are by different sculptors and were not designed as a pair.

Air Raids

Being a major port and the home of the Spitfire plane, Southampton was a target for German bombers. The first bomb fell on 19 June 1940 and the last, a V1 flying bomb,

The bombing of Southampton claimed 631 civilian lives.

or 'Doodlebug', on 15 July 1944. In total there were 2,631 high-explosive bombs and 30,652 incendiary bomb that were recorded. There were around sixty air raids that killed 631 people.

There is a memorial seat to these events in Hollybrook Cemetery. It is made out of the rubble following these raids on the town. Southampton lost 12.5 per cent of its housing stock, more than any other city in the UK. There were 3,589 buildings destroyed and around 40,000 damaged. The worst bombing was on the night of 30 November until the 1 December 1940.

Arcades

Following the French-led raid of 1338, the strengthening of the town's defence system was ordered by Edward III (1312–77). It was to be fully enclosed by a stone wall. This was especially along the Western Quays where wealthy merchants lived. The merchants were unwilling to lose access to their seafront warehouses and it took until 1380 before they became part of the town's defensive wall.

Left and previous page: Arcades built after the French raid of 1338.

Artesian Wells

Southampton's population grew in the nineteenth century, especially after the arrival of the railway in 1840 connecting the port to London. There was a need for a good water supply. The reservoirs on the Common were inadequate despite a well that was sunk to 1,260 feet. The scheme was abandoned in 1883. A new Southampton Waterworks was opened at Otterbourne in 1888.

Austen, Jane (1775–1817)

Austen's books, set among the English middle and upper classes, are notable for their wit, social observation and acute insights into the lives of early nineteenth-century women.

The Juniper Berry pub is now on the site where Austen once lived.

Born in the Hampshire village of Steventon, in 1801 the family moved to Bath. Jane's father died in 1805 and Jane, her sister Cassandra and their mother moved to Southampton in 1806. They lived here until 1809 at her brother Frank's house. The garden backed onto the medieval town walls but the original house no longer stands and the Juniper Berry pub now occupies the site. Jane attended Winter Balls at the Dolphin Hotel in the High Street, where she had also celebrated her eighteenth birthday. We know she saw plays at the former Theatre Royal in French Street and also visited Hythe using a hired boat.

Jane and her family worshipped at All Saints Church (once on the corner of High Street and East Street, destroyed during the Second World War).

In 1816, Jane began to suffer from ill health, probably due to Addison's disease. She travelled from her Chawton home to Winchester to receive treatment but died there on 18 July 1817.

Aviary

Well remembered by many older Sotonians, it was formerly situated in Andrew's Park. Situated near the Titanic Engineers Memorial, it was demolished in 1993 after existing for more than eighty years.

Bargate

In the Bargate on 16 January 1434, there were preparations for a great feast to be held in the Guild Hall upstairs by the Guild of Merchants. All the details and expenses for this are listed in the account book of the town steward, which is preserved in the City Archives.

The Bargate was the main entrance to the old town of Southampton. If you look up at the south side parapet you can see the seventeenth-century Watch Bell. At the

The Bargate dates from the late 1100s.

Above left: The lions are part of the legend of Sir Bevois.

Above right: George III.

Right: The Watch Bell dates from 1605.

end of each day, the Watch Bell (or curfew bell) was rung and the gate shut. Curfew derives from the French phrase *'couvre-feu'*, which means 'cover the fire'. Several taxes were collected at the Bargate by the broker. Two taxes were levied on carts: 'cartage' was paid on the cart and 'pontage' was a toll for using the bridge. There was also a 'Petty Custom' toll on goods carried. The earliest named broker was William Rede and in 1435 he collected £20 in taxes. The first floor of the Guild Hall was used as a courtroom and the ground floor was a prison.

The Bargate is a Grade I listed building originally built *c.* AD 1180. Further alterations were made to the building around 1260 to 1290.

In the middle of the four south side windows is a statue of George III (1738–1820) dressed as the Roman Emperor Hadrian, which replaced a wooden statue of Queen Anne (1655–1714).

The Bargate was separated from the adjoining town walls in the 1930s to enable trams to go around it. Southampton's Bargate has been judged by Pevsner as 'probably the finest, and certainly the most complex, town gateway in Britain'.

BBC Radio Solent

This local station was started in 1970 and was based in South Western House until 1991. Today it broadcasts along with BBC South from purpose-built premises in Havelock Road. Its slogan is 'Loving Life in the South'.

This building houses BBC TV South and BBC Radio Solent.

Beatles

Released on 30 May 1969, 'The Ballad of John and Yoko' was the seventeenth and final number one single record from the Beatles.

John Lennon's biographical lyric said:

> 'Standing in the dock at Southampton
> Trying to get to Holland or France
> The man in the mac said
> You've got to go back
> You know they didn't even give us a chance'.

The song was based on a real incident that happened at Townsend Thoresen ferries on 14 March 1969 at what is now Ocean Village.

See Southampton Facebook follower Kay has confirmed that her father-in-law Bill was 'the man in the mac':

'I asked Bill if he ever met any famous people at the ferries. Bill was in charge of the bookings and checked the cars in, documents etc. One night a chauffeur driven car (white Rolls-Royce I think) drove in and wanted to sail. They were not booked and didn't have their passports, Bill said no. Other staff were trying to get his attention and saying don't you know who this is? Bill still said no.'

Beckett, Joe (1892–1965)

Joe learned his trade as a fairground boxer, turning professional in 1912 and became the British Heavyweight Champion. His last fight was in October 1923 when he lost for a second time to Frenchman Georges Carpentier. Becket won thirty-one of his thirty-nine fights. One of his main opponents was 'Bombardier' Billy Wells, who Joe beat in 1919 to take the title.

Wells later went on to become the man who struck the gong at the introduction of the J Arthur-Rank cinema films. In retirement, Joe lived in Shanklin Road, near Hill Lane, Southampton.

Bell, Martin (1918–78)

Martin was educated at Taunton's School and then at the University College, now Southampton University. In 1967, he was appointed Gregory Fellow of Poetry at Leeds University.

He was unimpressed with Southampton's post-war reconstruction but, nevertheless, a number of Southampton's streets, buildings and monuments make an appearance in his poems. In 'High Street, Southampton', one of his finest poems, Bell makes reference to 'neat toy-town blocks of boxes, Noddy shops'. He went on to mourn the pre-war High Street he once knew, when it's 'shops packed in narrow cliffs rang joy'.

His best-known poems are the 'Enormous Comics' and a 'Letter to a Friend'.

Bevois Mount Murals and Plaques

Since 2016 the Bevois Mount History Group have organised four murals and five plaques in their area.

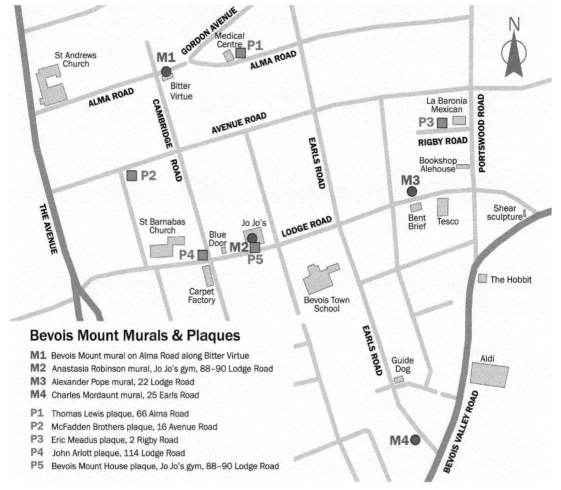

Bevois Mount Murals & Plaques

M1 Bevois Mount mural on Alma Road along Bitter Virtue
M2 Anastasia Robinson mural, Jo Jo's gym, 88–90 Lodge Road
M3 Alexander Pope mural, 22 Lodge Road
M4 Charles Mordaunt mural, 25 Earls Road

P1 Thomas Lewis plaque, 66 Alma Road
P2 McFadden Brothers plaque, 16 Avenue Road
P3 Eric Meadus plaque, 2 Rigby Road
P4 John Arlott plaque, 114 Lodge Road
P5 Bevois Mount House plaque, Jo Jo's gym, 88–90 Lodge Road

Graphic showing the locations of the Bevois Mount murals and plaques drawn by K. Lymer. (Kindly supplied by the Bevois Mount History Group)

Bevois Valley

An area of the city that takes its name from the medieval story of Sir Bevois. Published in 1502, 'The Romance of Sir Bevois of Hamtun' tells of Bevois, the son of Guy, Earl of Southampton, being sold by his evil stepmother Murdina, who had murdered Guy and ended up in Armenia.

He escaped and on his way home fell in love with the Princess Josian, was given a magic sword, Mortglay, and acquired a horse named Arundel.

After a battle with the giant Ascupart, two lions had killed his friend Sir Boniface and trapped poor Josian in a cave. She was saved from being eaten by lions because they were overcome by her beauty and ended up as her guards. Other versions say they were killed by Sir Bevois, who returned home to claim his birthright. The lions in front of the Bargate date from the 1740s and are a reminder of the tale.

Elements of the story are in Shakespeare's *Hamlet* and Disney's *The Lion King*.

Interestingly, Arundel Castle has a sword called Morglay, which may be a variant of Mortglay. In 1703 a tomb, said to be that of Sir Bevois, was found during excavations.

Blue Anchor Lane

During the 1300s this ancient lane connecting St Michael's Square to the West Quay waterfront was known as Wytegod's Lane after a wealthy merchant and mayor. He owned Tudor House and the property to the south side now known as King John's

Above and right: Blue Anchor Lane connects the former West Quay to St Michael's Square.

Palace. The lane carried goods from the west quayside up to the market square. Some say that ships moored there had a bluish hue to their anchors. The name Blue Anchor Lane was first documented in 1684. A Blue Anchor Inn was also located in the same lane. Today it looks like a quiet lane in the historic 'Old Town'. However, it was once densely populated and known as 'Piss Pot Alley'. This probably doesn't need any further explanation!

Boundary Stones

Historically, the town burgesses controlled an area enclosed by Hill Lane, Burgess Street (now Road) and the land west of the Itchen. Several of these old boundary stones survive; for example, the Rosemary Stone opposite No. 47 Burgess Road. Another, called the Hode Stone, is at the top of Hill Lane. In 1985 a council report, Beating the Bounds, proposed sites for a new set of stones at Redbridge, Old Bridge; Fernyhurst Lake in Rownhams; Lord's Wood Sports Centre, Itchen Valley; Cutbush Lane, Townhill Park; Netley Common; Tickleford Gully, Westwood; and Weston Shore. They were designed by the City Architect's department and show a rebus (a visual pun) with a S(outh) H(am) and Tun (a picture of a barrel), with an arrow pointing north on the top left and the year 1988 bottom right. The stone was recycled from the 'Old Rose Garden' formerly in Civic Centre Road.

Bradstreet, Ann (1612–72)

Puritan Ann stayed at the Star Hotel in the High Street while waiting to join the *Arabella* to sail to America from Southampton in 1630, just ten years after the *Mayflower* had left for the New World. Ann became the first published writer in England's new North American colony and was notable for her large body of poetry. Sheila Hancock, a Quaker who was born on the Isle of Wight, had 'To My Dear and Loving Husband' by Bradstreet read out at a memorial service for her husband, actor John Thaw.

> If ever two were one, then surely, we,
> If ever man were loved by wife, then thee;
> If ever wife was happy in a man,
> Compare with me ye women, if you can.
> I prize thy love more than whole mines of gold,
> Or all the riches that the East doth hold.
> My love is such that rivers cannot quench,
> Nor aught but love from thee give recompense.
> Thy love is such I can no way repay;

The heavens reward thee manifold I pray.
Then while we live, in love let's so persever,
That when we live no more, we may live forever.

Brutalism

Brutalist architecture gained popularity from the 1950s until the 1970s. It is characterised by simple geometric structures that often feature bare building materials, especially concrete. Beginning in Sweden, brutalist architecture is found around the world. The style has been most commonly used in the design of institutional buildings such as libraries, courts, public housing and city halls. It was used in the post-Second World War reconstruction of bomb-damaged Southampton.

Writer Owen Hatherley describes Wyndham Court, designed by brutalist architects Lyons Israel Ellis, as 'their masterpiece'. The building was meant to hint at the days of the transatlantic liners such as the *Queen Mary*. Near the Central station, it was finished in 1969 and was Grade II listed in 1999. However, its style has divided local opinion for over fifty years.

Wyndham Court was built in the concrete brutalist style and has underground parking.

Champion, Will (b. 1978)

Will is the drummer and backing vocalist for Coldplay. He was brought up in Highfield close to the University of Southampton, where his father, Timothy Champion, is an Emeritus Professor of Archaeology; his late mother, Sara, was also an archaeologist. Will attended primary school at Portswood Primary School, secondary school at Cantell Maths and Computing College, and then Peter Symonds College.

Churches

Medieval Southampton had five churches: St John the Baptist (in French Street until 1708); St Lawrence's (in the High Street until 1925); St Michael the Archangel, which is the only one remaining with parts dating back to 1070 and it has Southampton's oldest surviving parish records dating from 1552; Holy Rood in the High Street was bombed in 1940 and is now a Merchant Navy memorial; and All Saints at top of High Street, also bombed in 1940. Jane Austen worshipped there during her time in Southampton from 1806 to 1809.

The Mother Church of St Mary, with roots dating back to St Birinus in 634, was outside of the eastern boundary of the medieval town in the former Saxon settlement of Hamwic. In 1914 the sound of its then new bells inspired the popular song 'The Bells of St Mary's', later sung by Bing Crosby in the film of the same name. It recently had a new *Titanic* memorial window with bubbles representing those that died.

St Joseph's Catholic Church is situated on Bugle Street near Tudor. The church chancel was designed by Augustus Pugin and built in 1843. It was the first Catholic church founded in Southampton after the Reformation of the 1530s and is Grade II listed. Unusually, the church altar today lies on a north–west rather than east–west axis. The church contains a memorial table to the 'Italian Waiting Staff' who lost their lives on the *Titanic* ship.

Above left: Parts of St Michael's Church date from 1070.

Above right: The east window shows the five medieval churches of Southampton.

Right: The archangel Michael conquering evil.

This eagle lectern from 1320 was rescued from Holy Rood after bombing in 1940.

Clock Tower

In 1935, it was moved to the Bitterne Park Triangle. The tower had originally stood at the junction of Above Bar and New Road. It was bequeathed to the town in 1889 by Henrietta Sayers. The clock tower acted as a drinking fountain for both humans and horses. She also gave another fountain that was near the town side of the former Floating Bridge.

Coade, Eleanor (1733–1821)

Eleanor ran her own business from Lambeth in London making stone ornaments using her own brand of artificial stone. It has proved so hard wearing that many of her works remain in excellent condition today. The 1809 statue on the south side of the Bargate is a good example. It shows the head of George III placed on the body of the Roman Emperor Hadrian. More local examples of her work can be found in the gardens of Mottisfont Abbey near Romsey.

Cockerell, Sir Christopher (1910–99)

The inventor of the Hovercraft lived in Hythe for many years in Prospect Place. The theory behind one of the most successful inventions of the twentieth century was originally tested in 1955 using an empty cat food tin inside a coffee tin, an industrial air blower and a pair of kitchen scales. In June 1959 the world's first hovercraft SR-N1 took to the Solent. Hovercraft are still being built in Southampton at Griffon Hoverwork (Woolston). A memorial stone was erected in his honour at Hythe. Part of the inscription reads:

'Let this creative work be an inspiration to young engineers of the future'.

Court Leet

It is an ancient form of a local court. In the medieval period its jurisdiction covered the overseeing of standards in such matters as food and drink, weights and measures, agriculture and civic matters. Southampton still holds an annual 'Court Leet' in early October and is only one of a handful that still operate.

It originally met on 'Cut-Thorn Mound' on Southampton Common by the Bassett cross roads but was moved to the Guildhall above the Bargate in 1616. It moved to the former Audit House in the High Street in 1856. Court Leet continued there until the Law Court block of the Civic Centre was built in 1934. Today, it is held in the Council Chamber. A 'Beating the Bounds' ceremony, the ancient custom of clearing the markers of the town boundaries takes place before the annual Court Leet.

Cowherds

The Cowherd would take cows daily to the Common to graze. They would collect the animals from outside the Bargate and herd them up to the land that was owned by Lord Shirley until the town burgesses found against him in a land dispute in the 1200s. The Common was given up for the people to graze their livestock and to collect firewood, berries and peat. In 1767 the building we know today was built on the site of the old cowherd's house. In 1772 the holder of the post began to make and sell beer when Southampton was at the height of the spa town period.

Craven, Lady Betty (1750–1828)

The youngest daughter of the Earl of Berkeley married Lord Craven at sixteen. By 1780 the socialite Betty was in Southampton during its spa town period. In 1783 she met the married Margrave of Brandenburg. They had lived together as brother and sister until they were both free to marry. She had a house in Anspach Place, opposite the West Gate, until 1812. The Anspach name can be seen today in a stone plaque on the Pig in the Wall Hotel wall.

Crisp, N. J. (1923–2005)

Did you watch BBC TV series in the 1960s and '70s such as *Compact, Dixon of Dock Green, Dr Finlay's Casebook, The Brothers, Colditz* and *Secret Army*? They were all scripted by Southampton-born Norman James Crisp, known as N. J. Crisp, a prolific television writer, dramatist and novelist.

A manager for Southampton's Streamline Taxis, he went full time as a writer in 1959. He was one of several writers recruited to *Dixon of Dock Green* to rid the popular series of its previous 'cosy' image. Crisp also wrote for *Dr Finlay's Casebook* and in one episode he tackled the taboo subject of euthanasia.

The Expert (1968) about forensic scientist Dr John Hardy (Marius Goring) was the first BBC2 drama series to be made in colour. *The Brothers* (1972–76) attracted audiences of up to 11 million. Crisp also wrote scripts for *Colditz* (1972–74), the wartime prison camp drama.

In 1985 he wrote the play *Fighting Chance*, set in a rehabilitation centre, which was based on his own illness. He had a malformation of the spinal cord that left him partially disabled and was registered blind in the 1980s.

A founding member of the Writers' Guild in 1959, he later served as its chairman and negotiated the first £1,000 fee to be paid to a writer for a television drama. He lived in Abbot's Way in Highfield.

Cross House

Before the Itchen Bridge opened in 1977 passengers used the Floating Bridge (a cable ferry that crossed the River Itchen between Woolston and Southampton). The first Floating Bridge came into service in November 1836. Before then there was a ferry boat service. The Cross House, giving passengers shelter while waiting to be ferried across, survives and the present building dates from 1634.

D

D-Day Wall on Western Esplanade

Operation Overlord, launched on D-Day, 6 June 1944, was the largest military invasion in world history. Its aim was to liberate Europe from fascism and nearly a year later it succeeded with VE Day on 8 May 1945. On D-Day alone 156,000 Allied troops landed on the Normandy beaches.

Why was it called D-Day? Some say it stood for decision, departure or deliverance but for the US military it just was 'the day' when an operation started. So the day before

Below: Only this short stretch of red-brick wall remains.

Inset: Wonder what happened to Dave from Pennsylvania?

Maybe Bill survived?

or after was D-Day minus or plus one and so on. Likewise they used H Hour to refer to the time action would begin and had first used these conventions after entering the First World War in 1917. The British had originally used Z Day and Z Hour.

In July 1942 Combined Operations Military Movement Control and the Royal Navy Flag Officer had set up HQ in the South Western Hotel, which was known as the stone frigate HMS Shrapnel. The Southampton Area C also included Romsey, Winchester and Hedge End. The impact on Southampton was considerable as the American Army's 14th Major Port took over the town. A favourite haunt of US troops was the Gaiety cinema, Below Bar, where they would take local girls on a date. A Sprinkles Ice Cream parlour is on the site today. It was said at the time that the Americans were 'Overpaid, oversexed and over here!' The troops had chewing gum and local children were said to call out 'Got any gum chum?'.

Around 3.5 million British, American, Canadian and other Allied troops passed through on their way to France. There were around 2.25 million American troops in the Southampton area. Around 100 of their names, often with their hometown or state, survive on the 62-foot/19-metre wall carved by US troops waiting to depart from the nearby docks. In 2019 the Heritage Lottery Fund approved a bid led by the Maritime Archaeology Trust and supported by the See Southampton tour guides and others to digitally record the names and the stories behind them. Many of the young men who left their names would have been injured and some would have died on a Normandy beach. Their inscriptions are a poignant reminder of the sacrifices made during wartime.

Dibdin, Charles (1745–1814)

Southampton-born Charles was baptised in Holy Rood. He wrote music and words for over 600 songs and was well known in Georgian England. His patriotic songs were used as an aid to recruitment in the Napoleonic Wars.

He is misquoted for saying that a sailor has a girl in every port. He wrote, 'in every mess I find a friend, in every port, a wife'. In life he only sailed twice, both times to France, to escape creditors. A plaque to his memory is outside the remains of Holy

Above: Charles Dibdin wrote popular sea songs.

Right: Holy Rood is now a memorial to those who served in the Merchant Navy.

Rood Church. His best-known song was 'Tom Bowling', which is often featured at the Last Night of the Proms.

The former Conservative politician Michael Heseltine is a descendent and has 'Dibdin' as a middle name.

Disease

Southampton's medieval leprosy hospital dedicated to Mary Magdalen was situated near the present-day Civic Centre. The last warden of the hospital was pensioned off in the 1420s. There is information about leprosy on the corner of Watts Park, opposite the James Matthews building of Solent University.

In 1348, the Black Death arrived via a boat at Melcombe Regis near Weymouth. Southampton lost around 25 per cent of its population. Plague struck again in 1563 with around 400 deaths. The London Great Plague of 1665 spread to Southampton and

Around 180,000 people worldwide have leprosy, mainly in Asia and Africa, with around 100 cases a year diagnosed in the USA.

one estimate says 1,700 people died in over an eighteen-month period. The Mayor of Southampton appealed for help and Charles II sent the sum of £50, some doctors and 20 tuns of French wine. In 1849, cholera came to the town with some 200 people dying, mostly in Simnel Street, the Back of the Walls area and Kingsland. Further outbreaks in 1865 and 1886 led to forty-one and 100 deaths, respectively. From 1893 to 1921 Southampton had the *City of Adelaide*, built in 1864, as a floating isolation hospital ship off Millbrook Point.

The Spanish flu epidemic of 1918–19 also claimed many lives.

Dolphin Hotel

The original building dates from the early 1400s and its still-in-use cellars are original medieval vaults. During the late eighteenth century Southampton became a popular spa town. The Dolphin was rebuilt in 1775 to accommodate more visitors. Its bay windows are said to have been the largest in England at that time. When Jane Austen lived in Southampton from 1806 to 1809 she attended balls held at the Dolphin.

Below left: A bay window at the Dolphin Hotel.

Inset: Once many coach and horse carriages would have gone through here.

Below right: Jane Austen had her eighteenth birthday party at the Dolphin.

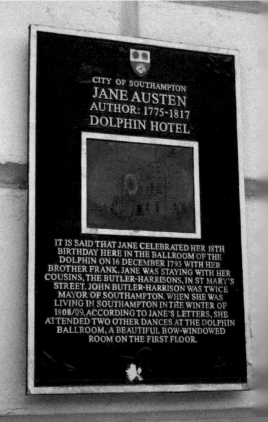

Dock Strike of 1890

In September 1890, dock workers in Southampton were seeking an agreement for union labour only to be employed in the docks and for agreement on wages. Their demands were not met and they had to concede and return to work only to find that the Royal Mail Steam Packet Company and the Union Steamship Company had granted concessions to the Seamen's and Firemen's Union.

Consequently angry dock workers intimidated other returning workers at the dock gates. The local magistrates, fearing that the police could not cope, messaged the Commander of the Portsmouth Garrison for military assistance. Two hundred and fifty men of the 19th Regiment and twelve officers arrived in Southampton in the evening and marched into Canute Road, where the dock workers had congregated. The mayor, Mr James Bishop, read the Riot Act, which authorised the authorities to declare that the group of twelve or more people had unlawfully assembled and had to disperse or face action.

Anyone assisting with the dispersal was indemnified if any of the crowd was injured or killed. After two hours of unpleasant street brawling, the fighting had not ceased, so the soldiers fixed bayonets and were ordered to charge the crowd. Several dockers were wounded by the advancing soldiers and the crowd quickly dispersed, leaving the rioters' leaders to be arrested and charged.

It is said that once the Riot Act had been read the monarch would not visit a place again. Queen Victoria never did.

Duke of Wellington Pub

This pub in Bugle Street is built on twelfth-century vaults. Benedict Ace, one of Southampton's first recorded mayors in 1237, was an early owner.

A timber-framed building was erected in the late 1400s when it probably became an inn. It was once known as the Bere House, then the Shipwrights Arms and later

Following wartime damage it was extensively renovated in the early 1960s.

Above: It is built on twelfth-century foundations.

Left: The Duke of Wellington in Bugle Street in the Old Town.

renamed in honour of Wellington's victory over Napoleon at the Battle of Waterloo in 1815. It was badly damaged by Second World War bombing and the rebuild was not completed until 1963. It is noted today for its summer hanging basket display.

Drink Map of Southampton

It was inspired by Revd Basil Wilberforce (1841–1916), who was rector of St Mary's Church, Southampton. Basil's eminent grandfather was politician and philanthropist William Wilberforce (1759–1833), who had campaigned for many years to abolish slavery. The drink map was published in 1878 by the St Mary's Church Temperance Society. It was designed to be handed out to the public in general and sailors disembarking from ships in Southampton Docks. Only one copy, in Southampton City Archives, is known to survive.

The intent was to highlight locations of temptation. These were shown as red spots on the map and indicated a licenced public house, whereby red stars indicated an alehouse. A teetotal sanctuary was identified on the far side of Brinton's Road. This was enforced by a covenant against public houses and alehouses.

The campaign was dropped as the map, far from being an aid to abstention, became a guide to those seeking the pleasures of alcohol.

E

Earhart, Amelia (1897–1937)

The aviation pioneer landed her plane on the River Itchen on 19 June 1928 near the 'Floating Bridge' in Woolston, Southampton, after becoming the first woman to fly across the Atlantic Ocean along with two men. She was met by Southampton's first female mayor, Lucia Foster Welch, and was given a civic reception. She later achieved the feat solo in 1932.

Amelia vanished alongside navigator Fred Noonan in July 1937 near New Guinea in the South Pacific as she attempted to become the first female pilot to fly around the world. Robert Ballard, who found the wreck of the *Titanic* in 1985, has attempted to find wreckage from her plane.

Echo

The local newspaper began in 1888. It once had offices in central Southampton that were where the entrance to the Westquay Shopping Centre is now. It publishes one edition each day except on a Sunday and started its online version in 1998.

Edward, the Black Prince (1330–76)

He was the son of Edward III. Both were in Southampton in 1346 on route to fight the French at the Battle of Crécy. The Prince Edward Tower was built around 1400.

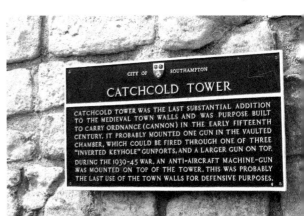

There was an anti-aircraft gun on top of Catchcold Tower in the Second World War.

Above left: Known as Catchcold Tower, this was one of the last additions to the medieval wall in the late fourteenth century.

Above right: Earlier defences had narrow slits for arrows but cannon shot was fired through here.

It is also known as Catchcold Tower and is an early example of a tower with keyhole gun ports for cannon to be fired from.

Eleanor of Aquitaine (1122–1204)

French-born Eleanor was one of the most notable females of the Middle Ages, with links to five kings. She reigned over Aquitaine for sixty-six years 358 days. When her marriage to Louis VII was annulled in 1152 in France she then married Henry II of England and had three sons, Henry, Richard and John, who all became kings.

At that time the trade of Southampton was based on wool out and wine in. Much came from her vineyards in Gascony and was stored in the town's vaults.

She devised the Rolls of Oleron in 1152, which set down much of maritime law. This was used in the Black Book of the British Admiralty still used today.

English Street

Following the Norman Conquest of 1066 the town was split into distinct parts. The victorious Normans took the desirable west with their houses fronting the water. The conquered Anglo-Saxons had the lower-lying east side of town. This division was shown in the use of French Street and English Street as road names. The latter is known today as the High Street, Below Bar. The Domesday Book of 1086 records ninety-six inhabitants of Southampton paying dues to the king, thirty-one from English Street and sixty-five from French Street.

F

Fiennes, Celia (1662–1741)

Celia was a pioneering female travel writer. She went around much of England on horseback from 1684 to 1703 and described late seventeenth-century Southampton as a quaint and pleasant town.

Freedom of the City

The honour of Freedom of the City is awarded to 'persons who have, in the opinion of the Council, rendered eminent services to the City'. It has its roots in medieval times when some important people were granted keys to come and go as they pleased through the town's gates.

Local footballers have been recognised in recent times such as Ted Bates (1918–2003), former player and manager of Southampton FC in 2001. Matthew Le Tissier (b. 1968) was awarded his Freedom in 2002. He only played for Southampton FC and was the first midfielder to score 100 Premier League goals and scored forty-seven out of forty-eight penalty kicks. He scored the last goal in the final competitive match played at The Dell on 19 May 2001, in a 3-2 win against Arsenal. This also turned out to be his last goal for Southampton FC.

Lawrie McMenemy (b. 1936), former manager of Southampton Football Club, was awarded his in 2007. This was followed in 2016 by Francis Benali (b. 1968), another former Saints footballer. He has raised over £1 million for Cancer Research.

French Raid of 1338

In 1337 the Hundred Years War with France began. It actually lasted 116 years. Early on Sunday 4 October 1338, fifty French, Genoese and Sicilians ships arrived. As the south and west of the town was not walled they landed around the bottom of Bugle Street. The town and its silver were looted and those citizens who took refuge in St Michael's Church were murdered there. One of the pirates was called Grimaldi and today that is the family name of the royal house of Monaco.

The western walls with some examples of medieval craft that would have traded here as the sea once came up to them.

There is a story of a Sicilian prince who when he encountered a club weilding Hampshire Yeoman, who came to take the town back, cried 'Rancon', meaning he would pay a 'ransom'. The yeoman took this as being 'Francon' or Frenchman and killed him with the club. As a result of the raid Edward III (1312–1377) ordered the town to complete its walled defences.

French & Son, W. J.

This traditional shoe shop in Bedford Place is one of the oldest businesses in Southampton. It has been located in Bedford Place since 1890. In 2019 it was awarded Independent Footwear Retailer of the Year. It has been run by eight generations of the same family. The average length of service for staff members is twenty-two years.

W. J. French & Son, an award-winning traditional shoe shop established in 1803.

Friary

Around 1224 a group of Friars Minor, who followed the teachings of St Francis of Assisi, came to the town. They were also called Greyfriars because of the colour of their robes. They settled in the poorer part of town near God's House hospice. They created a water supply for townspeople from Hill Lane via Conduit House (opposite the Mayflower Theatre) to their friary. In 1410 the town took over the system, making it the earliest urban water supply in England.

The friary was dissolved by Henry VIII in 1538. Today the site is occupied by the Friary House, an office building by the Gloucester Square car park.

The round tower remains. It was built in the late 1200s and was used as a dovecote. The honeycombs that you can still see in the base of the tower used to be the nesting holes for doves. The Friary Gate dates from when the eastern walls were built in the late 1300s as the friars were cut off from their orchards. They were allowed to build a gateway through the walls as long as they provided defences for the gate. The reredorter or dormitory was built in the late 1200s as a medieval en suite with a toilet block that could be reached from the dormitory. The waste fell down into a stone-lined drain that was washed clean by water from the adjacent tidal town ditch.

Garibaldi, Joseph (1807–82)

The Italian soldier and statesman who had been a leading figure in the fight for the unification of Italy visited Southampton on 16 April 1864 during his tour of England. A contemporary engraving shows his carriage surrounded by tumultuous crowds as it passed the Bargate. He spent the night at No. 27 East Park Terrace, home of the Southampton mayor, George Brinton. A tablet bearing the portrait of Garibaldi was later erected on the front of the house. It reads, 'dedicated by the Italian colony of Southampton to the memory of Joseph Garibaldi, the great father of the independence of Italy on the occasion of the centenary of his birthday, 4th July 1907'. The house, which became known as Garibaldi House, was demolished after the Second World War and the tablet was removed to Tutor House Garden.

Gilbert's Bookshop

This unique bookshop was founded in 1859. From 1939 it was situated at the unusually numbered No. 2½ Portland Street, off Above Bar. It ceased trading in 2002.

Gonella, Nat (1908–98)

Nat was a jazz trumpeter known as Britain's 'Louis Armstrong'. He spent time in Southampton in the 1940s and 1950s, living at No. 18 Norwich Road, off Woodmill Lane, Southampton. He played regularly at the Court Royal Hotel in Southampton. Nat Gonella is said to be the trumpet player on Lew Stone's 'My Woman' in 1932. This was sampled and speeded up in 'Your Woman by White Town' (1997). This led to a number one single.

General Gordon (1833–85)

Born in London, he served in the Crimea in 1855 but made his name in China with a British Expeditionary Force that fought its way to Peking. He was Governor of the Sudan from 1873 to 1880 and went back in 1884 to put down a revolt led by the Mahdi, a religious leader. He became trapped in Khartoum and a relief force arrived two days after his death. Victorian Britain saw 'Chinese Gordon' as a popular hero. When in Britain he stayed in Southampton with his sister at No. 5 Rockstone Place. A monument in Queens Park commemorates him. Interestingly, it does not have a statue of him on it as he disapproved of such displays of vanity.

Above left: Regency buildings in the Bedford Place area.

Above right: Where General Gordon stayed with family members when in Southampton.

Right: He was referred to as Chinese Gordon and Gordon of Khartoum.

Hamwih/Hamwic/Hamtun/Hamwith/Hamtune

All these are variants of names given to pre-Norman Conquest (1066) Southampton. Unusually, the Roman (Clausentum), Saxon and Norman towns were on different sites. Hamwih was founded around 690 by Ina, King of the West Saxons, whose capital was Winchester. The Vikings raided Hamwih in 840 and 842. In 962 Hamwih was first referred to as Suthamtune perhaps to distinguish it from the Mercian Hamtune, now called Northampton.

Harriott, Joe (1928–73)

Born in Kingston, Jamaica, Harriott was a noted jazz alto saxophonist and composer. He came to the UK in 1951 and recorded from 1954 and 1969. He worked with most of the well-known jazz musicians in the UK and was compared to Charlie Parker. He is particularly known for developing fusion jazz, including incorporating Indian music into jazz.

Joe lived in London, but often played at the Concorde Club, Eastleigh, and the former Blue Indigo Club in Southampton. He was in Southampton when he was admitted to hospital with cancer and died in January 1973. He is buried in the churchyard of Holy Saviour, Bitterne. The epitaph on his gravestone is in his own words: 'Parker? There's

Jazz saxophonist Joe Harriott is buried in Bitterne, Southampton.

them over here can play a few aces too'. He had said this to remind people that there were great jazz musicians in the UK as well as in the USA. There is a Black History Month plaque to him near Southampton Guildhall just down from Guildhall Square.

Hodsoll Report

There was a report by Sir John Hodsoll, Inspector General of Civil Defence, on the bombing of Southampton in 1940 with comments by local politicians Sir James Matthews and Mr Rex Stranger. It criticised civic leaders for poor planning.

There was consternation in the 1970s when it was declassified and said that people had left the city in droves. The Mass-Observation Survey taken on 4 December 1940 recorded that the people of Southampton were 'Broken in spirit' and that from 4.30 p.m. in the afternoon there was a steady stream of people leaving the heavily bombed city to sleep in outlying areas.

Holyrood Church, the Sailors' Church

It was badly bombed in 1940 and its shell now remains as a memorial to those who served in the Merchant Navy. The original twelfth-century church stood further out into the High Street. It was moved back in 1320 to its present site. The troops leaving for Crécy in 1346 and Agincourt in 1415 would have prayed here before departing.

In 1554 Philip of Spain prayed here on route to Winchester Cathedral where he married Queen Mary. He also brought in the new custom of exchanging gold rings.

The date of the Quarter Jacks who strike every quarter of an hour is unknown but they were mentioned in 1760 and said to be old already.

Richard Taunton's tomb is at the rear of the church. The nave has a gravestone to John Speed, descendent of the great Elizabethan local map maker of the same name. The Ten Commandments are carved on the end wall and state that we should commit no murder rather than the more commonly used 'Thou shalt not kill'.

Its rare Brass Lectern dating from around 1350 with wings open was rescued from the burning church during the height of an air raid in 1940 by the churchwarden, Mr Blake, and a soldier. It is now in St Michael's Church. It was painted dark brown and is regarded as a good example of an eagle in wood until the paint was scraped off. It is believed that it was painted so Cromwell's men would not steal it during the English Civil War (1642–48).

Just inside the church you will find a Titanic Memorial Fountain, which is dedicated to the firemen, stewards and crew from Southampton. It was paid for by the families and friends of the lost crew. The memorial was originally erected further north on Cemetery Road as a drinking fountain on 27 July 1915. It was moved to its current location in Holyrood Church on 15 April 1972 –the sixtieth anniversary of the sinking of the *Titanic*.

Above left: 'MN' above the entrance stands for Merchant Navy.

Above right: Holy Rood was badly bombed in November 1940.

Left: This drinking fountain was originally on Southampton Common.

Below: The *Titanic* had four funnels as shown in the carving.

THIS MEMORIAL FOUNTAIN
WAS ERECTED IN MEMORY OF THE CREW,
STEWARDS, SAILORS AND FIREMEN,
WHO LOST THEIR LIVES IN THE S.S. TITANIC DISASTER.
APRIL 15th 1912
IT WAS SUBSCRIBED FOR BY THE
WIDOWS, MOTHERS AND FRIENDS OF THE CREW.
ALDERMAN HENRY BOWYER MAYOR 1912–1913
REMOVED FROM THE ORIGINAL SITE IN CEMETERY ROAD,
THE COMMON.   15th APRIL 1972

Above: Money was raised by the widows, mothers and friends of the crew.

Below left: An anchor from the *QEII*, which left Southampton for the last time in 2008.

Below right: Cunard ships still call at Southampton.

ANCHOR FROM QUEEN ELIZABETH 2 (QE2)
DONATED TO THE CITY OF SOUTHAMPTON BY CUNARD IN MARCH 2010,
TO COMMEMORATE THE LONG ASSOCIATION BETWEEN THE CITY
AND THIS ICONIC LINER. THE QE2 LEFT HER HOME PORT
OF SOUTHAMPTON ON HER MAIDEN VOYAGE IN MAY 1969 AND WAS
A FAMILIAR SIGHT IN THE PORT, CARRYING PASSENGERS
TO NEW YORK AND MANY OTHER DESTINATIONS.

IN 1982 SHE SERVED IN THE FALKLANDS WAR, AS A TROOP SHIP
AND HELICOPTER CARRIER. HER FINAL VOYAGE WAS IN
NOVEMBER 2008 WHEN SHE RECEIVED A HUGE AND EMOTIONAL SEND
OFF FROM THE PEOPLE OF SOUTHAMPTON.

Hythe Pier

It was opened in 1881. A hand-propelled narrow gauge railway was built on the pier in 1909, and was electrified in 1922. The rolling stock consists of two four-wheeled electric locomotives built by the Brush Electrical Engineering Company in 1917. Originally they were battery powered and were used in the mustard gas factory in Avonmouth during the First World War.

Invasion

Southampton had a vital role in the D-Day preparations, with two-thirds of the initial British Assault Force leaving from here in June 1944. Southampton became Military Area C with the town, in effect, sealed off to civilians.

The trees on either side of the Avenue are said to have been originally planted following the English victory led by the Duke of Cumberland over the Jacobite forces of Charles Edward Stuart at the Battle of Culloden near Inverness in 1746. During the Second World War they were allowed to grow over, forming a tunnel to hide the road from the air. Many original trees were lost to the Dutch elm disease outbreak in the 1970s.

The Mulberry Harbour, which played a pivotal part in Operation Overlord, was built here in Southampton. In the King George V Graving Dock some of the outer protecting bombardons were assembled. The whole unit was towed by some 200 tugs to Arromanches where some parts still remain. The 'Pipeline Under The Ocean' (PLUTO) was also constructed in Southampton. It provided a supply of oil to our forces.

Italians

English wool was in great demand in Europe by the late 1200s, especially in northern Italy. The Italians sent ships directly to England from 1305. The great galleys from Florence and Venice brought prosperity to the town.

The Venetians sent a yearly fleet with spices, wines, glass, silk, dates, olive oil and ivory and took back fine fleeces.

The volume of trade meant some Italians settled here. The Florentines adopted St. John's Church and the Venetians St Nicholas's chapel, which stood somewhere near St Mary's. The Genoese used the Friary near God's House. A Venetian, Gabriel Corbet, became sheriff in 1453 and a Florentine, Christoforo Ambruogi, became mayor twice.

J

Jellicoe, John (1859–1935)

Born in Southampton in Cranbury Terrace, Jellicoe was educated at Banister Court School, joined the Navy and became a captain in 1897. He became Commander of the Grand Fleet in 1914 and engaged with the German fleet at the Battle of Jutland on 31 May 1916. He became First Sea Lord in 1917. From 1920 to 1924 he was Governor of New Zealand and was created Earl Jellicoe in 1925. On 8 September 1925 he opened the Dock Board offices at Town Quay and was also present at the opening of the first phase of the Civic Centre in 1932. Jellicoe is buried in St Paul's Cathedral, London.

Jesus Chapel

Built in 1618 and consecrated in 1620, Jesus Chapel was the first church in England to be consecrated after the Protestant Reformation. Situated on Peartree Green, it was originally built as a chapel of ease for the trans-Itchen districts of St Mary's Church in Southampton, hence the name St Mary Extra. The original peartree pip is said to have been planted by Elizabeth I. It also contains a memorial stone in the grounds to Richard Parker. He was from nearby Itchen Ferry Village and was shipwrecked in a boat with two others in 1884. In order to survive they drew lots and Richard was the subject of cannibalism.

(St) Julian's

Gervaise le Riche was a very wealthy merchant who built God's House in 1185. It provided assistance to pilgrims from France on their way to Canterbury. These pilgrims needed a chapel in which to worship and he named it after the patron saint of travellers. It is said to have had a window for lepers who were not allowed in but could view a service.

The chapel in Winkle Street is said to contain the headless body of Richard, Earl of Cambridge, who was beheaded after the Southampton Plot against Henry V in 1415. Every July a public service is held in French.

Juniper Berry

Author Jane Austen (1775–1817) lived in a house that was on the site of the present-day Juniper Berry pub in Upper Bugle Street. After the death of her father in Bath she, her sister and mother moved to Southampton and lived with brother Frank from 1806 to 1809. Her time here is thought to be behind these words in Mansfield Park: 'the effects of the shadows pursuing each other on the ships at Spithead and the island beyond, with the ever varying hues of the sea, now at high water, dancing in its glee and dashing against the ramparts...'

This mock-Tudor pub was once popular with merchant seamen.

K

Kimber, Sidney Guy (1873–1949)

Notable local politician Kimber was born in Southampton on 5 November, hence his middle name. Educated at King Edward VI Grammar School, he took over the family brick business in Highfield in 1900. In 1910 he was elected as a Conservative councillor and was influential in local politics for many years. Mayor from 1918 to 1920, Kimber was involved in ensuring the completion of Southampton's Cenotaph. This was designed by Sir Edwin Lutyens, who also designed the one in Whitehall.

In 1929 he helped to purchase Northam Bridge for the expanding town, abolishing the tolls. He arranged for the Floating Bridge to come under civic control in 1934.

A major force behind the building of the Civic Centre, the clock tower was locally known as 'Kimber's Chimney'. He and architect E. Berry Webber are said to have tied a balloon to the site and then driven around the town to make sure the tower, when built, could be seen far and wide.

Kimber was also behind the building of the Sports Centre and Municipal Golf Course in Bassett/Lordswood. Knighted in 1935, he died in 1949 and is buried in Highfield Church.

This plaque commemorating Sidney Guy Kimber is on the first floor of the Civic Centre.

King George V Graving Dock

This former dry dock is situated on reclaimed land in Southampton's Western Docks. It was formally opened by George V and Queen Mary on 26 July 1933. The first ship to use the dock in 1934 was the White Star Line's *Majestic*. Built specifically for the new large liners coming into service, like the RMS *Queen Mary* and RMS *Queen Elizabeth*, this dry dock was once the biggest in the world. When full it held 58 million gallons of water and took four hours to empty. The dock also proved useful when the Mulberry Harbours were put together for D-Day in 1944.

King John's Palace

This building is known as King John's Palace as it was believed that King John (1166–1216) stayed in it during the early 1200s. Wealthy Norman merchants built their houses on the western shore of the town. Built around 1180, the house was ideally located on the quayside where ships loaded and unloaded their cargoes. After the French raid in 1338, Edward III ordered the completion of the town walls and the building was integrated into the walls. Although now only a shell, King John's Palace is one of the finest surviving examples of Norman architecture in the country. When No. 79 High Street was being demolished following bomb damage during the Second World War, a rare Norman chimney was found. In 1953 it was resited at King John's Palace.

Below left: The remains known as King John's Palace are through the arch on the right.

Below right: The arch was part of St Denys Priory.

This cannon is said to have been given by Henry VIII.

Kitchener, Lord (1850–1916)

On a visit to Southampton in 1902 Lord Kitchener was made a Freeman of the Borough. He became a national hero after reconquering Sudan in 1898, avenging the death of General Gordon. He is remembered for his 'Your Country Needs You' poster to aid recruitment of the armed forces in the First World War.

Local pride in Southampton of his success was manifested in the naming of a number of streets in his honour. This included Khartoum, Omdurman and Kitchener Roads in the area of Portswood. Kitchener died when HMS *Hampshire* sank in 1916. His name is on the Hollybrook Memorial, which remembers the names of nearly 1,900 people who 'have no grave but the sea'.

Krays

During the Second World War when Reggie and Ronnie Kray were children, their mother took them away from the Blitz in London to the relative safety of Hampshire. Later when things got a bit too intense in the East End, the twins would come down to Hampshire for a break. Here Ronnie could play lord of the manor with his silver-topped cane and tweeds, while he and his brother Reggie would drink in their favourite pub outside of London, The Bugle, near the waterfront in Hamble.

The twins bought a small house in the village, Hamble Manor Lodge, right next door to Hamble Manor. They are rumoured to have had various dealings with the local underworld in Southampton. There are stories of a motor launch that was owned by the twins being abandoned at Southampton Docks when they were finally imprisoned. 'Mad Axeman' Frank Mitchell was said to have been wrapped in chicken wire, weighted down, and dropped in the Solent after he was murdered by the Krays' associates. There are also stories of a collection from a bank manager in Waterlooville of £85,000 that was taken to Ronnie Kray while he was in prison.

La Rue, Danny (1927–2009)

The singer, entertainer and female impersonator lived in Southampton for twenty-one years. He had a house in Bassett Green Close and then lived in the Riverdene flats at the Bitterne Park end of Cobden Bridge. His 1987 autobiography was called *From Drags to Riches* but after a failed property investment he lost £1 million.

Lawrence of Arabia (1888–1935)

From 1894, a young T. E. Lawrence spent several summers at the former Langley Lodge on the edge of the New Forest. In 1929, now known as Aircraftsman T. E. Shaw, he helped organise the Schneider Trophy that took place off Calshot and again in 1931. There is a plaque on the wall of Lawrence House that is now part of Calshot Activities Centre. He then helped Hubert Scott-Paine at the British Powerboat Company in Hythe. He oversaw the construction and trials of high-speed power boats for the RAF. He lodged at Myrtle Cottage on Shore Road in Hythe, which today has a blue plaque. He also had lodgings in the now demolished Birmingham Street in Southampton.

La Sainte Union (LSU)

After the 1789 French Revolution Catholic education was limited by the state. In 1826 the order of La Sainte Union des Sacre Coeurs (LSU) was founded to promote Catholic education in France. From 1829 the attitude to Catholics in England was more tolerant with the Catholic Emancipation Act. In 1830 the first post-Reformation Catholic church in Southampton, St Joseph's, was opened. In 1880 the Sisters of La Sainte Union arrived in Southampton. They purchased Archers Lodge and opened the Convent High School for boarders in 1881. In 1904 a day school, St Anne's, was opened.

In 1899 the Sisters had opened a teachers' centre, which became a female residential teacher training college in 1904. Later La Sainte Union became LSU and accepted students of all faiths and none.

The site was taken over by Southampton University when the teacher training courses ceased in 1997 and was renamed New College. It is currently a residential development, incorporating some of the original Grade II listed buildings.

Livingstone, David (1813–73)

The noted African explorer and missionary was seen as a Victorian hero. He was the first European to see the feature he named the Victoria Falls. In 1866 he set out to find the source of the Nile and had lost contact. The *New York Herald* sent reporter Henry Morton Stanley to find him, which he did on 10 November 1871, saying 'Dr Livingstone, I presume?' His embalmed body arrived at Southampton in 1874. He had died the previous year. It is said it was kept overnight at Holy Rood before being taken to the Terminus station to go to Westminster Abbey, London.

Long House

In Porters Lane, situated near the Town Quay, are the remains of a Norman building around 111 feet long. As the tax was based on the front of the houses, the buildings were usually narrow and long. Long House is also known as 'Canute's Palace'.

This Norman building dates back to the early twelfth century.

The name was first given to the building by Sir Henry Englefield (1752–1822) in his 1801 publication *A Walk Through Southampton*. He wrongly suggested it was where King Canute ordered the tide back. The name 'Canute's Palace' is not accurate, as King Canute was crowned in 1016 and was not alive when the house was built in the early 1100s.

Before the town walls were built (after the French raid in 1338) its doors opened straight on to the shore. The ground floor was the warehouse area. You can still see the supports on the wall where the lanterns or candles used to stand. The first floor was reached by external stairs.

The windows on the top floor are rounded and of typical Norman architecture, which is a sign that the owners used to be wealthy. The western end gable is still at full height, but a lot of it was reconstructed.

Lucas, Richard Cockle (1800–83)

The eccentric Lucas exhibited busts, medallions and mythological scenes at the Royal Academy between 1829 and 1859. He lived for most of his adult life in a house named 'The Tower of the Winds' in Chilworth, and was a friend of Lord Palmerston, who lived at nearby Broadlands. David Lloyd (*Buildings of England: Hampshire and the Isle of Wight*) wrote: 'Not much sculptural work by him seems to survive but what there is, is good.' He is best known locally for his statue of Isaac Watts from 1861.

In 1909 one of his pieces was mistaken for a work by Leonardo da Vinci. This was the wax bust of a girl entitled *Flora*, based on a painting of the same name by Leonardo. A number of experts assumed the bust to be by Leonardo too, but it was actually made by Lucas in 1846. He was in the habit of driving through Southampton in a vehicle that resembled a Roman chariot, dressed in a Roman toga. His most eccentric trait, however, was a belief in fairies. His son, Albert Durer Lucas (1828-1919), lived at No. 50 Padwell Road in Southampton. Also a notable artist, a number of his oil paintings are in Southampton Art Gallery.

Lyster, Sir Richard (*c.* 1480–1554)

Sir Richard was the Lord Chief Justice of England during the reign of Henry VIII and Chief Baron of the King's Exchequer from 1546 to 1552. He married Isabel, the widow of Sir John Dawtrey (collector of customs under Henry VII) and lived with her in the building now known as the Tudor House Museum. He attended Queen Anne Boleyn's coronation. He also took part in the trial of Sir Thomas More and was Henry VIII's divorce lawyer. Following his first wife's death, he married again. When Richard Lyster died his widow erected a tomb to him in St Michael's Church.

Matthews, James (1887–1981)

The eldest of nine children, James was offered a scholarship to Cambridge University in 1913, but did not take it. From 1921 he was the first secretary of the Southern District Workers Educational Association (WEA), and from 1924 this was his full-time job. He became a co-opted member of the Southampton Borough Education Committee in 1930. He stood as a Labour candidate in the local elections unsuccessfully five times before being elected in 1934. He remained a councillor until 1945, when he became an alderman. He was active on the Education Committee and in town planning from 1945 to 1967, and influential in the post-war rebuilding of Southampton. He helped to get the city permission to build the Itchen Bridge. He was involved with the Open University from 1969, and also on Southampton University committees. He was knighted in 1966.

Matthews played an important role in the post-war reconstruction of Southampton and was knighted in 1966.

Mayflower

Southampton was the place that the various groups of pilgrims and others first joined together. Sixty-five passengers in all joined the ship here. The *Mayflower* dropped anchor in Southampton Water on 27 July. For seven days she waited for her sister ship, the *Speedwell*, which was on its way from Delfshaven, Holland, with fifty Leyden church members.

The memorial on Town Quay, Southampton, opposite Mayflower Park was unveiled in 1913 and has plaques telling the pilgrims' story. The memorial, with a replica of the ship on top, marks their possible departure point. John Alden, a Southampton cooper (barrel maker), sailed with the pilgrims when they eventually left on 15 August 1620.

The *Speedwell*, despite two refits, was still leaky. The pilgrims had to put in at Dartmouth for further repairs. Then, when they were 200 miles beyond Land's End they had to turn back for Plymouth because *Speedwell* sprang another leak. The *Speedwell* was deemed too unreliable to attempt an Atlantic crossing. Nearly all the pilgrims crammed on to the *Mayflower* and, once again, set sail. The *Mayflower* was not a large ship, just over 100 feet long and weighing 180 tons.

The abandoned *Speedwell*, with all her leaks, was sold soon after the *Mayflower* left for America. After yet another refit she continued to make many profitable voyages. There has

This monument marks the departure of the *Mayflower* from Southampton in 1620.

been a certain amount of speculation around this fact. Some say Master Reynolds, the captain of the *Speedwell*, was afraid of the Atlantic crossing and purposely made the leaks himself. There is also a view that Plymouth was not the last English port the *Mayflower* put into. Allegedly she stopped off at Newlyn in Cornwall for fresh water supplies.

In April 1621 the *Mayflower* sailed for England and she arrived in Rotherhithe in May. Within the year Captain Jones was dead at fifty-two. By 1624 she was unseaworthy. No one knows what became of her hulk.

Southampton is proud of our part in the pilgrims' story and our *Mayflower* connection. We have a Mayflower Park on the shoreline close to the spot where the *Mayflower* departed. Our impressive theatre, close to the main railway station, is called The Mayflower. Through Dock Gate 10 there is a Mayflower Cruise Terminal, and one of the University of Southampton's halls of residence is called Mayflower Halls.

McFadden, Frank (1856–1933)

On the 1871 census, Frank, aged fifteen, was living with his family at Norma Cottage in Avenue Road, Southampton. For many years Frank was employed as an engraver for the Ordnance Survey, which was then in London Road.

He is remembered for his drawings of Southampton in the late nineteenth century. Frank's best-known work was 'Vestiges of Southampton'. This was published in 1891 and was a collection of twelve etchings, including views of the West Gate, St Michael's Church and Tudor House. Many of his drawings were based on photographs by his contemporary, Thomas Hibberd James, and are therefore largely factually accurate. On several occasions he exhibited at the Royal Academy in London.

Meadus, Eric (1931–70)

Eric was an artist with a distinctive style and was born in Rigby Road, Portswood. His family soon moved to Lobelia Road on the newly built Flowers Roads Estate, which is situated off Burgess Road, Southampton. Eric attended Bassett Green School and won a scholarship to King Edward VI Grammar School. When Eric left school he became an apprentice draughtsman at Vickers Armstrong before doing National Service and emigrating to Canada for two years. He then obtained employment as a draughtsman for Pirelli Cable Works. He continued to work there until the end of his life. Many of Eric's paintings feature houses and other buildings in the Swaythling area of Southampton in the 1950s and 1960s. His work is often compared with that of L. S. Lowry, with whom Eric was acquainted.

Eric died at the age of just thirty-nine years old. He was just beginning to achieve a degree of fame in the art world. Eric Meadus Close by Swaythling railway station is named after him.

Around 4 per cent of Southampton's population are Muslim.

Medina Mosque

Medina Mosque opened its doors in 2001 as the first purpose-built mosque in the south of England.

Merryfield, Buster (1920–99)

In 1940 Buster, later well known as Uncle Albert in *Only Fools and Horses*, was posted to Southampton as a bombardier in the Royal Artillery. He was billeted in King Edward VI Grammar School and doubled as a fitness instructor, taking his charges on runs across the Common. He also helped in clearing up the town during the Southampton Blitz.

Mogshed, Little and Big

These are the unusual names of the two coppices on Southampton Common. They are near the great loop off The Drive at the north-west corner of the Common. Big Mogshed lies north/north-west of the Ornamental Lake. Little Mogshed joins at the north-west extremity. The name (properly Mogshade) signified a moist (muggy) shelter for grazing animals.

Mix, Tom (1880–1940)

American Tom was a cowboy actor in silent films. He is said to have ridden his horse from Southampton Docks into the foyer of the South Western Hotel in 1926.

Mitchell, R. J. (1895–1937)

In 1913 Noel Pemberton Billing set up a company to produce seagoing planes. The company was located in Woolston and Mitchell joined in 1916, becoming chief engineer in 1920. Supermarine aircraft won the coveted Schneider Trophy for sea planes in 1927, 1929 and 1931. The expertise gained from this was incorporated into the design of the new Spitfire plane, with the first one flying from Eastleigh on 5 March 1936. Mitchell died of cancer before the first plane was delivered to the Air Ministry. His story was told in the film *The First of the Few* (1942), with Leslie Howard playing Mitchell and David Niven as test pilot Geoffrey Crisp. Supermarine Spitfires played a critical role in the Battle of Britain in 1940. A prime target, the Supermarine works were destroyed by bombing on 26 September 1940. Over 22,000 spitfires were built but it is estimated that only 179 remain. Mitchell and his wife lived in Portswood and both are buried in a simple grave in South Stoneham Cemetery.

Mountbatten, Earl (1900–79)

The bronze statue was presented to the city in 1990 by developers after some restoration work on houses in Grosvenor Square. The 9-foot-high statue is by New Forest sculptor Greta Berlin. Lord Mountbatten lived at Broadlands in Romsey and had close connections with Southampton. He was the first patron of the City of Southampton Society between 1963 and 1979. Solent University Library is also named after him.

Earl Mountbatten was seen as the royal with the common touch. He had been the last Viceroy of India before independence in 1947.

National Liberal Land Company

It was responsible for developing Bitterne Park and Bitterne Manor in the late 1800s. In 1882 the company bought 300 acres of land lying west of Midanbury Lane on which they laid out a series of new roads including Cobbett Road, Cobden Avenue, Whitworth Crescent and Road, Thorold Road and Bullar Avenue. The stated aim was 'to provide homes with proper sanitary arrangements, thus promoting health and longevity'. An advert describes the estate as the most convenient and charming suburb of Southampton. There are pubs such as the Hop Inn and the Bitterne Park Hotel at the estate edges but deliberately none on it to promote temperance.

The company also built Cobden Bridge, opened in 1883, to link their new estate with the centre of Southampton. In 1893 the company dropped the word 'Liberal' from its title, but its original political identity is obvious from the names chosen for the new roads.

Northam Bridge

In 1796, David Lance held a meeting to propose a bridge over the River Itchen to take stagecoaches from Southampton to Portsmouth. By 1799 a timber toll bridge was completed. The wooden bridge was replaced in 1889 by an iron bridge. Tolls were ended in 1929 when the town acquired it. The present structure dates from 1955 and was the first major prestressed, precast concrete road bridge to be built in the United Kingdom. Cables were stretched with winches and concrete poured over them. They were gradually let go as the concrete hardened.

Oakley and Watling

This Southampton High Street company supplied the fruit and vegetables to the *Titanic* on its maiden voyage in 1912. Alfred Oakley is listed in the 1843 directory with a market garden based in Love Lane, now St Mary's Road.

Robert Oakley is listed in 1845 and 1847 directories as 'Seedsman' and greengrocer, with premises at No. 122 High Street. By the 1850s, Alfred Oakley & Son, market gardeners, are listed at No. 118 High Street. Henry William Watling first appears in Southampton street directories in 1871. The firm was named Oakley and Watling from around 1874.

The O and W are still visible over 100 years after Oakley and Watling supplied the *Titanic*.

The business moved across the road to No. 56 High Street by the Red Lion pub in 1908, where they traded until 1975 when the company was taken over by Southern Ship Stores.

October Books

In 2018 Southampton's leading independent bookshop moved into the old NatWest bank in Portswood Road. It was only a short way from their previous premises and reflecting its values as a not for profit and cooperative organisation, they gained much publicity from using a human chain to move stock.

Old Bonded Warehouse

It was designed with a planned canal in mind but the canal scheme collapsed in 1808. Originally a flight of steps ran down from the building to the proposed canal with a recess in which barges could be loaded.

The Old Bond Store represents a lost building type for Southampton where such stores were once commonplace. A lease from 1820 indicates it was used as a builder's store. An 1868 map shows the nearby eastern town walls had been pulled down. That map also states its purpose as a malt house, possibly for the nearby Coopers Ales Brewery. It overlooked All Saints Church graveyard, which is today the site of a multistorey car park.

Old Cemetery

In 1843 an Act of Parliament was passed enabling a cemetery to be opened on Southampton Common. It was consecrated in 1846. Among its graves is that of Lt Col. Hewitt, the last surviving officer to have fought at the Battle of Waterloo in 1815. He died in 1891 aged ninety-six.

Many Belgians fled to England during the First World War and there are a number buried in Southampton cemetery. There are also over sixty graves of people connected to the *Titanic* disaster. The Friends of Southampton Old Cemetery are a volunteer group who work to record and maintain it.

Old Farmhouse

Situated by the Mount Pleasant level crossing, the Grade II listed Old Farmhouse former pub once stood in open fields. A brick records the date of the present building as 1611 but some parts date to 1560. It is thought Oliver Cromwell (1599–1658) and/or his son Richard stayed there. Richard had married Dorothy Major, a grand-daughter of a former Mayor of Southampton. The couple lived in Hursley Park, near Winchester. This is currently used by IBM.

Richard Cromwell (1626–1712) briefly followed his father as Lord Protector of England in 1658/59 and is buried in Hursley church graveyard. The Old Farmhouse pub was reportedly haunted by a young Irish girl. A skull was found in a cellar and was displayed behind the bar. It ceased trading in early 2019.

Ordnance Survey (OS)

It was formed in 1791 to carry out a military survey of England and was based in the Tower of London. In October 1841 a devastating fire there led to the Survey moving to military barrack premises in Southampton at the junction of the Avenue and London Road. Once the orphans of soldiers were housed there and this is commemorated by the name Asylum Road. The military connection ended in 1870. Later in 1968 it moved to Maybush until 2010 and was once a major local employer. The site now has the Compass housing development. The OS has since moved to new premises off the M271 in Explorer House, Adanac Drive.

Below left: The OS moved to the Barrack Block in 1841.

Below right: Names of OS staff who lost their lives in both world wars.

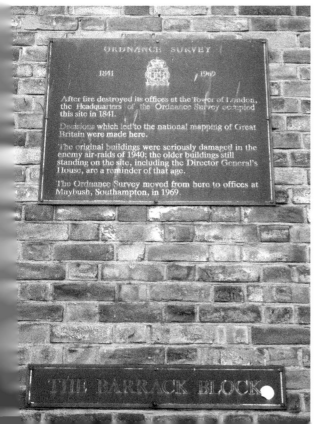

Paganini

On the evening of 30 August and morning of 31 August 1832, the world-famous virtuoso violinist Nicolo Paganini (1782–1840) gave two concerts at the Long Rooms in Southampton to nearly a thousand people in total. He gave up giving public concerts in 1834. The flamboyant Paganini was thought by some to be 'The Devil's violinist'. Philip Klitz (1805–54) a brilliant performer on the pianoforte and violin, conducted Paganini's concerts in Southampton. He was the organist of St Lawrence's and St Joseph's churches in Southampton, and from 1845 to his death of All Saints Church, just below the Bargate.

Palmerston (1784–1865)

Viscount Palmerston was born at Broadlands, Romsey, and he has a statue there in the Market Square. He became a popular Foreign Secretary and later in 1855 he became Prime Minister. He was a burgess of Southampton and on his death in 1865 a memorial committee was set up to collect money from the public. A statue was unveiled in 1869 in what was then called Fair Field, now known as Palmerston Park. The sculptor Thomas Sharp of London was promised £800 for the commission but was not paid in full and took legal action against the committee.

Parks

Southampton's 'Jewel in the Crown' is its impressive amount of green spaces, second only in size to those in Sheffield. Watts, Andrews, Houndwell, Hoglands, Palmerston and Queens parks were once Lammas lands. The word 'Lammas' derives from 'Loaf Mass' when bread was made from the first sheaves of wheat harvested and a blessing is given. The fields were owned by the hereditary burgesses of Southampton from Candlemas (2 February) to Lammas Day (1 August). They were divided into strips for growing foodstuffs. After 1 August the fences were removed and the land used for animal pasture. In the 1850s the land was bought by the council from the burgesses

Above left: The lime tree walk through the parks.

Above right: The statue of former coachmaker and mayor Richard Andrews.

Right: The avenue of trees were presented by Mayor Perkins in 1862.

THIS AVENUE OF TREES
WAS PRESENTED TO THE TOWN
BY THE LATE
SIR FREDERICK PERKINS
DURING HIS MAYORALTY
IN 1862

and turned into parks. The Victorians believed that parks provided opportunities for walks, recreation and sport that would improve public health.

In 1862 Mayor Frederick Perkins presented the town with the beautiful avenue of lime trees that stretches to this day from Andrews (East) Park through Palmerston Park toward Houndwell.

Paris Smith

This legal firm can trace its local roots back to 1818. In 1912 they were representing Captain Smith in a dispute over his previous ship RMS *Olympic*. He was one of more than 1,500 who perished in the *Titanic* disaster.

Permaloo, Shelina

She was born in Southampton to parents from Mauritius. Shelina is a cook, author and winner of the *MasterChef* TV competition in 2012. In *MasterChef* her final menu was octopus served on marinated fennel and ginger; mutton curry with chilli pumpkin roulade and mango cannelloni filled with lime curd. Her first book *Sunshine on a Plate* contained recipes inspired by Mauritius. Shelina opened her first restaurant Lakaz Maman in Bedford Place, Southampton, in 2016.

Pink Floyd

The group played their first gig without founder Syd Barrett (1946–2006) at the Student's Union of the University of Southampton on 26 January 1968. T-Rex, who at the time were an acoustic duo of Marc Bolan and Steve Peregrin Took (who took his name from a hobbit in *Lord of the Rings* and was a friend of Barrett), were also on the bill. Pink Floyd's 1975 song 'Shine On You Crazy Diamond' was about Syd as that was his nickname. Barrett is also thought to have appeared on some of Took's solo songs such as 'Syd's Wine'.

Polymond Tower

This once hidden tower in the north-east corner of the Norman and medieval town is now more accessible with the Bargate Quarter development. It was originally owned and maintained by St Denys Priory as a 28-foot-high structure but fell into disrepair.

Nine times mayor, John Polymond rebuilt the tower in the 1360s. However, records from 1654 tell of Polymond Tower again being in disrepair because being near the town ditch its foundations were insecure. This was a poor part of the town and during the 1665 plague some destitute families lived in it. In 1828 the council proposed to tear down the whole building but after an outcry the current one-storey tower remains.

Pope, Roger (1947–2013)

Drummer Roger played for Elton John's band in the late 1960s and early 1970s. He was on the Elton and Kiki Dee hit 'Don't Go Breaking My Heart' and several of Elton's early albums. In the mid-1960s he had been in local band the Soul Agents, who had a young Rod Stewart as their singer. Roger was also best man at The Who drummer Keith Moon's first wedding. He is said to have turned down the chance to play for Paul McCartney's Wings.

Portal, Henri de (1690–1747)

Portal was born in 1690 in France into a Huguenot family. They were French Protestants who were inspired by the writings of John Calvin. Louis XIV broke the charter that protected their religious freedoms forcing half a million Huguenots to leave France for Protestant countries. It is said that the Portal family were facing torture and in their flight from France Henri and his brother Guillaume were smuggled out of France in wine barrels. They eventually found refuge in Southampton. The Huguenots brought many new skills with them and in Southampton found an established French community who, with the permission of Elizabeth I in 1567, had used St Julian's Chapel in Winkle Street. Even today it is known as the French Church and public services are still held there in French once a year in July.

In 1705 Henri was employed at South Stoneham Mill to learn his trade as a papermaker. In 1711 he gained the tenancy of a mill near Whitchurch. In the same year Henri became a naturalised citizen and from then on was known as Henry Portal. In 1718 he obtained the Laverstoke Mill between Whitchurch and Overton.

In 1724 the Bank of England asked him to make the paper for British banknotes. The business continued until it was acquired by the De La Rue Company in 1995.

Queen Victoria

On 8 July 1833 she formally opened the Royal Pier, accompanied by her mother, the Duchess of Kent. Queen Victoria had Osborne House on the Isle of Wight built as her and Prince Albert's summer retreat. In 1843 Queen Victoria and Prince Albert arrived at the Terminus station to go on a marine excursion on the royal yacht *Victoria and Albert*. For some reason the royal yacht had not been brought close to the pier so that Victoria had to step on to her barge. To get her there dry-footed, the mayor and aldermen took off their official robes (being scarlet) to make a pathway for the queen. When the Crimean War came to an end she ordered a military hospital to be built. Netley was chosen as the site because it was near to Southampton, allowing hospital ships from around the

It took ten hours for coaches to get to London. A young Victoria stayed here.

The gatehouse to the former Royal Pier.

British Empire to safely disembark patients. The foundation stone was laid by Queen Victoria on 19 May 1856. The jetty by the hospital was specially built for her visit and a scarlet carpet covered the walkway. This occasion was marked by the firing of a royal salute. Unfortunately one gun fired prematurely and two sailors were killed. The laying of the foundation stone ceremony still went ahead. Beneath the stone a copper casket was placed containing the plans of the hospital, the first Victoria Cross, a silver Crimea medal with all four campaign bars and a set of British coins.

On 26 July 1890 Queen Victoria arrived to open the Empress Dock. It is rumoured that the Southampton Corporation sent Queen Victoria a bill for the red carpet laid down for her at the ceremony. Maybe this is the reason that she never returned to Southampton again?

Queens

The *Queen Mary*, named after Mary of Teck, the wife of George V, had her maiden voyage to New York from Southampton on 27 May 1936.

During the Second World War, the *Queen Mary* and her sister ship *Queen Elizabeth* were used as troop ships. Hitler offered an Iron Cross to any U-boat commander who sank either ship.

In 1967 the *Queen Mary* finally left Southampton for Long Beach, California, where she remains. The RMS *Elizabeth* was named after the wife of George VI and later Queen Mother. During conversion to a floating university she sadly caught fire and sank in Hong Kong harbour in 1972. Her successor the *QEII* was also a troopship during the Falklands War in 1982. Today she is in Port Rashid, Dubai. An anchor from her is outside of Holy Rood in the High Street.

Today the Queens in the Cunard fleet are *Queen Mary II* (2,691 passengers), *Queen Elizabeth* (2,081) and *Queen Victoria* (2,061).

Red Lion

This High street pub started life as a medieval merchant's house and still retains its fourteenth-century vaults. The central area is a fifteenth-century open hall called Henry V's Courtroom. In his play, Shakespeare sets the 1415 trial of the conspirators against Henry V here but it is more likely to have taken place in Southampton Castle.

The Red Lion claims to have a number of ghosts.

Rostron, Captain

RMS *Carpathia* made her maiden voyage in 1903 and ran the Cunard service from New York to a number of the Mediterranean ports. The *Carpathia* was sailing from New York on the night of 14 April 1912 under Captain Arthur Rostron when he was woken by his telegraph operator. Harold Cottam had contacted the *Titanic* at 12.11 a.m. and received in reply a distress signal. Captain Rostron closed down all services that used steam from the boilers and under maximum speed set out to assist the *Titanic* at her last known location some 58 miles away, reaching her four hours later. After working her way through hazardous ice fields the Carpathia took aboard 706 people from lifeboats. The last person to come aboard the *Carpathia* was the *Titanic's* 2nd Officer Charles Lightholler. Later the thankful survivors presented Rostron and crew a cup and a gold medal.

George V gave him a knighthood and USA President Taft presented him with the Congressional Gold Medal. Rostron retired from sea life in 1931 and recalled his life story in *Home From The Sea*, which is a highly collectable book. Rostron's home was at Chalk Hill, West End, in Southampton, a house built on land owned by Herbert Collins and built in the Collin's familiar architectural style. It is said that the rear of the house was designed to remind Rostron of a ship's bridge. Rostron died in November 1940 and his funeral took place at West End Parish Church.

Rolling Mills, Weston

Weston Grove House was built in 1801 and demolished in 1941. It was due to be sold in 1909 to the London & South Western Railway for the construction of a proposed large dry dock. The *Titanic* and a sister ship, owned by the White Star Line, were being built in Belfast. This dry dock was meant to be for their use when they came to Southampton but the project did not go ahead.

The Weston site was sold to the Ministry of Munitions and the Rolling Mills were built in 1914 to make ammunition during the First World War. The main building had 12-foot-thick foundations and a flimsy wooden roof to ensure that any accidental explosion would be directed upwards and cause less damage. The half-a-mile-long Rolling Mills employed many women during the First World War, driving the gantry cranes and using machine presses to produce the brass discs for shells. Employees worked a sixty-five-hour, seven-day week (half a day on Saturday). They earned £3 for a flat week, £4 with maximum overtime.

The building was badly bombed during 1940 and 1941. In 1942 the Royal Navy moved in, building part of a Mulberry Harbour on the foreshore outside the depot. The site closed in 1986 and was badly contaminated so the present housing development was delayed until the area was deemed safe.

Romans

In AD 43 the Emperor Claudius decided to conquer Britain. Four legions were sent and one legion commanded by Vespasian moved west from Kent and the port of Clausentum was established on the east side of the River Itchen. Some scant remains can still be found in the Bitterne Manor area.

Traces of Roman roads to Winchester and Chichester have been discovered as has an altar stone to Ancastra, a local God. After the Romans left in AD 410 the Saxons arrived and set up the settlement of Hamwih on the other side of the River Itchen around the area of the present-day St Mary's Stadium.

Ropewalks

Rope was made by attaching hemp to a special type of wheel with hooks. The hemp was fixed to a horse, which was then made to walk along a pathway, the wheel was made to turn and the yarn was made. Rope walks could be up to a quarter mile in length. Five rope walks have been identified in eighteenth- and nineteenth-century Southampton. Joseph Clark of St Mary's Road was one of the leading ropemakers in Southampton in the mid-nineteenth century. Today the Ropewalk Community Garden in Derby Road recalls this lost skill.

Russell, Ken (1927–2011)

Southampton-born Ken attended Taunton's School. Some of his films, including *The Devils* (1971) and *Lisztomania* (1975), were considered to be vulgar. However, his adaptation of D. H. Lawrence's *Women in Love* (1969) and *The Boyfriend* (1971) were both well received. His film of The Who's rock musical *Tommy* (1975) was popular and well suited to his extravagant style.

S

Sandell, Elsie (1891–1974)

One of Southampton's best-known local historians, she was a prolific writer, producing a number of books on the town's history, including *Southampton Cavalcade* and *Southampton Panorama*. She also wrote a range of booklets on local history for children, articles for the *Daily Echo* and often spoke on radio and television. Elsie helped organise the D-Day memorial embroidery completed in 1953. She lived at Winn Road from 1923 to 1970 and a block of flats in The Parkway, Bassett, was named Sandell Court in her honour.

Shinn, Don (b. 1945)

In the 1960s Southampton organ and keyboard player Don backed Dusty Springfield and Rod Stewart. He has worked with many musicians including Elkie Brooks, Kiki Dee, James Taylor and Engelbert Humperdinck. Keith Emerson from Emerson, Lake and Palmer (ELP) acknowledged him as a major influence on his keyboard style.

Shrapnel, Major General (1761–1842)

Born in Bradford on Avon, Wiltshire, Major General Shrapnel died at Pear Tree House in Southampton. The shell that bears his name was recommended for use by the Army Board of Ordnance in 1803. The Duke of Wellington used it during the Peninsular War. The Commander of the Artillery wrote to the Duke: 'The shell is admirable to the whole army and its effects dreadful'. The Shrapnel shell proved very effective during the Battle of Waterloo in 1815. Henry Shrapnel was promoted to regimental colonel in 1814 and was given a life pension. He was then promoted to major general and retired from active service in 1825. He originally lived in Bugle Street but moved to Pear Tree House in the mid-1830s. Today we think of shrapnel as meaning the flying fragments of material that come from the shell rather than the shell itself. He is buried in the family vault at Holy Trinity in Bradford on Avon.

Southampton Castle

Very little remains visible of the once splendid Southampton Castle. Today only part of the outer bailey wall survives and along the outer wall by the sea there is Castle Vault and Castle Watergate, as well as the remains of Castle Hall and the Garderobe (latrine tower).

It was constructed as a Norman-style motte-and-bailey castle, which consisted of a wooden keep situated on a raised earthwork called a motte, accompanied by an enclosed courtyard, or bailey, surrounded by a protective ditch and palisade. The palisade was replaced by a stone curtain wall in the first half of the twelfth century.

Henry II took steps to improve the condition of the castle and the wooden keep was converted into a stone shell keep. The castle played an important role in the wine trade, and Castle Vault was built to store the king's wine, just beneath the keep at the quayside.

One of Southampton's wealthy merchants, Gervase le Riche, paid a part of Richard I's ransom after his crusades. In 1194 Richard 'the Lionheart' spent his only Christmas in England as king at Southampton Castle. During the early 1200s King John increased spending on the castle, which was by then completely built in stone. Southampton Castle was equipped with its first cannon in 1382, making it one of the first in England to be equipped with the new weapon. The castle declined again in the sixteenth century and Elizabeth I was the last monarch to visit it, saying it was the worst castle she had ever stayed in. The castle was sold off to property speculators by James I in 1618. In 1804, the ruin was bought by the Marquis of Lansdowne, who built a Gothic mansion on the site. This was demolished around 1818 and by 1902 the site was flattened by commercial developers. A tall block of early 1960s flats now stands on the area.

These early 1960s flats are on the site of the original castle, which lasted until the early 1600s.

Rear view of Castle Way flats. The mural on the wall was originally at Sainsbury's in Lordshill and depicts key events in Southampton's history.

Southampton Football Club

Today's professional football team can trace their roots back to 1885. The nickname 'Saints' comes from its formation as St Mary's Church of England Young Men's Association team. In 1898 they moved to the Dell in Milton Road and to the present 32,500-capacity St Mary's Stadium in 2001.

The Saints anthem is 'When the Saints Go Marching In', a traditional tune popularised by Louis Armstrong. Unlike other teams that use the tune the original lyric is not changed for the Saints.

Saints were defeated in the FA Cup finals of 1898 and 1902, finally winning 1-0 against Manchester United in 1976. Their highest ever league finish was second in the old First Division in 1983–84. Southampton were relegated from the Premier League in May 2005, ending twenty-seven successive seasons of top-division football for the club. Southampton returned to the Premier League for the 2012–13 season.

Southampton Terrier of 1454

This was a comprehensive survey of all properties in the medieval town. The names of the owners and some past owners are given and those of their tenants. Its purpose was to allocate for each property responsibility for the maintenance of a specific section of the town wall.

South Western Hotel

Work began on the South Western Hotel in 1865. Designed with a strong French influence, it was originally named the Imperial when it opened in 1867. Many of the first-class passengers on the *Titanic* stayed there. This building was once Southampton's grandest hotel and it is now a Grade II listed building.

In 1942 it became the HQ for Military Movement Control in readiness for the Normandy landings and was known as the stone frigate HMS Shrapnel. Winston Churchill and General Eisenhower had a meeting at the hotel.

Many Wrens were billeted there and one in particular was Rozelle Raynes, who wrote *Maid Matelot* in which she recalls her wartime memories of Southampton and the infestation of the hotel by cockroaches. Post-war it became South Western House, being used by the BBC for local radio and television production. The shipping line Cunard was also located in the hotel. With the opening of the new BBC buildings in Havelock Road, Southampton, the hotel was converted into luxury flats.

The former Wedgewood Ballroom of the hotel has been converted into a bar, bistro and restaurant named the Grand Café.

Soper, William (*c.* 1390–1459)

Using Watergate Quay and the nearby 'Canute's Palace' as a storehouse, Soper was commissioned to build a number of vessels by Henry V, including the *Grace Dieu*. Begun in 1416 and launched two years later at 1,400 tons, it was the largest ship to have been built in England at that time. Soper's ships were moored in the River Hamble, which provided a safe anchorage. Soper had other skills, notably as a diplomat and politician. He was elected to the House of Commons eleven times. He was also twice Mayor of Southampton. Following the death of Henry V in France in 1422 Soper was paid to bring back his body, and was later involved with escorting Henry VI's bride-to-be Margaret of Anjou across the channel prior to their wedding at Titchfield Abbey. The role of Keeper of the King's Ships was held until 1442, though the fleet itself had declined following the death of Henry V. Soper then took up an appointment as a New Forest Verderer, looking after the Royal Hunting Grounds.

Speedway

Speedway racing was first held at Banister Court Stadium in 1928. The original idea, when the land was purchased in 1927, by fishmonger Charles Knott, was to build a greyhound racing track, but it was soon decided to add a speedway track. The stadium was very near the former Hampshire County cricket ground in Northlands Road. It was also minutes from the previous home of Southampton FC at the Dell. Their most successful season was in 1962 when they won the National League Championship. The Banister Stadium closed a year later and was demolished in 1964. Today Charles Knott Gardens is in the area and is named after both father and son of the same name. The younger Charles Knott played cricket as a bowler for Hampshire, taking 647 wickets.

St Mary's Church

Southampton's mother church, St Mary's (the site dating from a visit by St Birinus in AD 634 to convert the Kingdom of Wessex to Christianity), is situated outside the later Norman town in the earlier Saxon settlement of Hamwih.

Victorian expansion led to a new church being built in 1878 with Edward, Prince of Wales, laying the foundation stone. This was destroyed by bombing on the night of 30 November 1940. The current building, the sixth on the site, dates from 1956.

The church bells are said to have inspired the famous song 'The Bells of St Mary's' as sung by Bing Crosby in the 1945 film of that name.

Star Hotel

The Star in the High Street is built on medieval foundations and was used as an inn by the 1600s. The present façade dates from the late 1700s and was refurbished in 2016.

The Star was a popular coaching inn with regular services reaching London in ten hours. In 1831 the future Queen Victoria stayed there with her mother.

Stella Memorial

The Stella Memorial was erected on the Western Esplanade in 1901 by public subscription in memory of stewardess Mary Anne Rogers. She gave her life in the sinking of the passenger steamship *Stella* on Maundy Thursday 30 March 1899. The *Stella* was owned by London & South West Railway, the train company that ran a service from London Waterloo to the Channel Islands via Southampton. They were in competition with the Great Western Railway, which ran a service from Paddington to the Channel Islands via Weymouth. The Channel Islands' ports, St Peter Port and St Helier, were only large enough to berth one ship at a time, so the rival companies often raced to get into harbour first. On Maundy Thursday 1899, both companies advertised a special steamer service arriving in Guernsey at 5:30 p.m.

The *Stella* left Southampton with 147 passengers and forty-three crew but ran into heavy fog. As he did not want to arrive second, Captain Reeks maintained full speed. Shortly before 16:00, the fog signal from the Casquets Lighthouse was heard. Although the captain attempted to turn away from the rocks, *Stella* scraped along two rocks, and then her bottom was ripped open by a submerged granite reef.

The *Stella* sank within eight minutes and eighty-six passengers died, along with nineteen crew.

Mary Anne Rogers distributed lifebelts to the women and children and guided them into the boats. She even gave up her own lifebelt to a young girl who had lost her mother and refused to get into one of the overcrowded lifeboats.

Her reported last words were, 'Lord, have me'. Her body was never found.

Following the disaster the two steamship companies finally agreed to run services on alternate days so that there would be no more racing. In 1973 the wreck of *Stella* was discovered by Channel Islands divers south of the Casquets.

Stonehouse, John (1925–88)

John Stonehouse is remembered for an unsuccessful attempt to fake his own death in November 1974. He tried to escape financial problems by leaving a pile of clothes on a Miami beach. Obituaries were published but no body was found. In fact, married John had gone to Australia with his secretary Sheila Buckley. Australian police originally thought he may be Lord Lucan, who had disappeared just two weeks before.

Stonehouse conducted his own defence during a sixty-eight-day trial in 1976. He was sentenced to seven years in prison for fraud, resigned as an MP and declared bankrupt.

His mother Rosina was Mayor of Southampton in 1959. John was educated at Taunton's College, joined the Labour Party at sixteen and in the 1960s became a Minister of State for Technology and later Postmaster General. It has since been revealed that he had been a known Czech spy since 1962, though no prosecution was made. John had a series of heart attacks at home in Totton and died in hospital in April 1988.

T

Taylor, Walter (1743–1803)

Walter supplied wooden rigging blocks to the Royal Navy, greatly improving their quality. His work has been noted as a major aid in Nelson's sea victories such as the Battle of Trafalgar during the Napoleonic Wars. His father (also named Walter) had previously served at sea and had observed the problems caused by traditional hand-carved blocks, which would often jam during the heat of battle.

Taylor and his father developed machinery to mass-produce rigging blocks to an exact standard. He also offered a 'guarantee' to replace any that failed. One of Taylor's other inventions, important in the block-making process, was the circular saw. In 1781 Taylor moved to Woodmill where there was a better supply of water and room to power some of the equipment by steam engines.

Taylor was the sole supplier of blocks to the Royal Navy from 1759, supplying some 100,000 a year until his death in 1803. He is buried at South Stoneham Church.

Taylor's original premises were at the Westgate.

Above: Plaque to Walter Taylor.

Left: Many have passed through the Westgate including those who boarded the *Mayflower* in 1620.

Terminus Station

Stagecoach travel slowly declined with the coming of the railway. In 1840 the London & South Western Railway arrived with the line reaching the newly opened Terminus station, designed by Sir William Tite.

The large South Western Hotel (originally the Imperial Hotel) was added and the line was extended into the docks to allow boat trains to terminate on the quayside. Notably many passengers about to depart on the ill-fated *Titanic* in 1912 would have arrived here and spent their last night on land in the South Western Hotel. However, by the 1960s, largely due to modern aircraft travel, the liner trade had declined and the Terminus railway station closed in 1966. Now a casino, the platforms have been removed and all that remains is the huge glass canopy. Southampton Central (formerly Southampton West) is now the main railway station in Southampton.

Thomas, George (1853–1907)

George was 'the man who built The Dell', Southampton Football Club's home prior to the move to St Mary's Stadium in 2001. The club began as St Mary's Church of England Young Men's Association FC in 1885 and quickly became a major force in local football. They had begun recruiting professionals by 1892 and joined the newly created Southern League in 1894. They moved home from the Antelope Cricket Ground to the Northlands Road County Cricket Ground in 1896. It was during the initial season there that Saints won their first Southern League title. They repeated the feat and reached the semi-finals of the FA Cup in 1897–98. The Dell opened in

September 1898 with covered stands on both sides of the pitch, which seated over 4,000 (only Villa Park in Birmingham had more).

The stadium was in a natural dell created by the Rollsbrook, a stream that rises on the Common. It had originally been excavated to accommodate goods sidings for the aborted Didcot, Newbury & Southampton railway line. The Dell was an expensive undertaking and Thomas charged rent of £250 per annum for use of the ground. Market Chambers in the High Street was purpose built by George Thomas as the HQ of his business empire. When Southampton's first telephone exchange was opened in 1886 Thomas had two lines installed –there were only three other subscribers.

The first match at the Dell was a Southern League fixture against Brighton United on Saturday 3 September 1898, which Saints won 4-1. The last ever Dell game was a friendly against Brighton & Hove Albion on 26 May 2001, with Saints winning 1-0. After the game, at the invitation of the club, many fans took home their seat and other souvenirs.

Tides

Southampton has a famous 'double tide', each tide rising for up to seven hours, followed by an ebb tide of less than four hours. The 'double tide' has been put to good use throughout Southampton's history. Southampton Castle built its garderobes, or latrines, in the fourteenth century on the west shore so that waste could be swept away by the tide.

During the Second World War Southampton was Britain's number one military port, and the long hours of high water meant that more troops could board vessels over a shorter period of time than at other ports. This was of particular importance during the D-Day embarkations.

Time Ball

Today we take access to accurate time for granted but this was not always the case. Not all timepieces have clock faces and a time ball can relay accurate timing to ships in port, which is necessary for navigation. Although latitude on the globe could be calculated via the sun's position, longitude was only possible with the invention of accurate maritime timepieces that could be carried aboard ship, thus allowing mariners to calculate speed and therefore distance from their home port.

A time ball was installed on the roof of the South Western Hotel by the London & South Western Railway and Harbour Board from 1904 as a visible sign for nearby ships to regulate their chronometers.

It worked by way of receiving an electrical impulse from Greenwich at 10.00 a.m. and the ball, some 5 feet in diameter, would then drop down the mast. Prior to being on the South Western Hotel it was previously located on the top of God's House tower from 1888.

Titanic

Her ill-fated maiden voyage from Southampton starting on 10 April 1912 still captures the imagination of people all around the world. The 269-metre-long Belfast-built *Titanic* was operated by the White Star Line, who had moved to Southampton in 1907. One of her four funnels served a purely aesthetic purpose, since four funnels were considered more pleasing to the eye than three. She only had enough lifeboats for around a third of the people on board but this was within the legal requirements of the time.

Times were hard in 1912 in Southampton. The National Coal Strike meant that many were without work that April. Only the White Star Line was recruiting crew for their new luxury liner. They had been able to gather sufficient coal from other vessels and suppliers. The majority of White Star crew were signed on for one voyage at a time. Many came from the poorer areas of the town such as Chapel and Northam. *Titanic*'s arrival also meant a boom for local firms, as for example F. G. Bealing's nursery at Highfield provided 400 plants for the ship and buttonhole flowers for every first-class passenger. *Titanic* struck an iceberg at 11.40 p.m. and sank at 2.20 a.m. on 15 April. A total of 2,224 sailed and 1,517 people died.

Above: Plaque to the postal and telegraphic workers on the *Titanic*.

Left: Memorial to the *Titanic*'s engineers.

Above left: Recently plaques have been put on some of the homes of crew lost on the *Titanic*.

Above right: Millvina Dean was the youngest and last *Titanic* survivor.

The tragedy had a devastating effect on many Southampton families. Out of the total of 897 crew members, 715 men and women had their home address in Southampton and only 175 returned home alive. More than 500 families not only lost a loved one but often also their main source of income. In Southampton *Titanic* relief funds were organised for the families of lost crew members, raising nearly £450,000 (around £20 million in today's money). However, even though the financial consequences could be dealt with, the emotional scars ran deeper. Widows had to cope without their husbands, children had to grow up without their fathers and many survivors struggled to come to terms with the fact they had lived while many others had perished.

The Band That Played On

Of all the many acts of heroism on the night the *Titanic* sank, none has captured the public's imagination quite like that of the band that played on the liner's deck to maintain calm on board. A memorial concert at the Royal Albert Hall, in May, 1912, was hailed as the 'greatest professional orchestra ever assembled' and was conducted by (later Sir) Thomas Beecham, Sir Henry Wood and Sir Edward Elgar.

The musicians Wallace Hartley, John Woodward, Theo Brailey, Jock Hume, Roger Bricoux, Percy Taylor, Georges Krins, and Fred Clarke were employed by an agency CW & FN Black, who held a monopoly on providing band members for passenger ships. Band leader Wallace Hartley's body was recovered and returned to Liverpool on board the White Star Line ship *Arabic*. His violin was found strapped to him and sold at auction in 2013 for a reported £900,000. The bodies of Jock Hume and Fred Clarke were also found and buried in cemeteries in Halifax, Nova Scotia.

This replica plaque to the *Titanic*'s musicians is on the premises of legal firm Paris Smith. The original was destroyed by wartime bombing.

Tudor House

This is Southampton's original museum opened in 1912. The main structure was developed by Sir John Dawtrey, MP for Southampton in 1495 and Sheriff of Hampshire in 1516. Richard Lyster, Lord Chief Justice of England from 1546 to 1552, lived here. The gardens contain a cannon said to be given to the town by Henry VIII in 1543. There is also an arch from St Denys Priory and a plaque to the Italian nationalist Garibaldi, who visited Southampton in 1864.

Tudor House was opened as Southampton's original museum in 1912.

U

Union Castle Line

The Union Steam Ship Company started a monthly mail service in 1857. It merged with the Castle Line in 1900. Until 1965 a Union-Castle ship left Southampton at 4.00 p.m. every Thursday. It then became a Friday 1.00 p.m. departure until services ceased in 1977.

Universities

Southampton today has two universities: the University of Southampton and since 2005 Solent University. Combined they attract at least 44,000 students to the city. In 1850 Henry Robinson Hartley left £104,000 in his will to found an institution for the study of natural history, astronomy and antiquities. It was disputed by relatives and £34,000 was spent on lawyers' fees. The Hartley Institute was finally opened in the High Street in 1862. An early treasurer was William Erasmus Darwin, the eldest child of Charles Darwin. It became a university college in 1902 with degrees awarded by other universities. By 1914 new buildings were built at Highfield but were taken over as a military hospital during the First World War. The original Hartley buildings were demolished in 1936. In 1952 the university college became an independent university. An adjacent road is named Hartley Avenue.

Solent University's main campus is in East Park Terrace.

Vaults

Estimates of the number of medieval vaults vary from forty-eight to sixty. One fine example is at No. 94 High Street. It is a barrel vault constructed around 1320 and may have once been a shop. Along with others this vault was used as an air-raid shelter in the Second World War and bunk beds were fitted. The relatively low number of 631 civilian deaths during the air raids is attributed to locals using these ready-made shelters.

Below left: The quadripartite roof and fireplace in the undercroft.

Below right: A carving that is thought to be Edward III.

Plaque on the Undercroft vault.

Quilter's vault in the High Street.

Inside No. 94 High Street.

Above left: Lankester vault.

Above right: Lankester vault ceiling.

Victoria Cross

One of the earliest awarded VCs was to Sotonian George Day in 1857. In 1918 Lieutenant Commander Marcus Beak, an Old Tauntonian, was awarded one. A memorial paving slab to him is in front of Southampton Cenotaph.

Southampton Cenotaph.

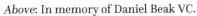

Above: In memory of Daniel Beak VC.

Right: Spitfires on the side of the James Matthews building of Solent University.

Below: Plaque to James Brindley VC in Guildhall Square.

The children's play area at the corner of the sports centre is in memory of Jack Mantle (1917–40), who was educated at Taunton's School before joining the Royal Navy. He was in charge of the gun ship *Foylebank* in Portland Harbour when German aircraft attacked on 4 July 1940. Jack was badly wounded but kept firing till he died and was posthumously awarded the Victoria Cross. Only 1,358 have ever been awarded.

Vikings

Viking raids on Southampton and the Kingdom of Wessex during the eighth and ninth centuries disrupted trade with the Continent. Important industries that were previously well established in Saxon Hamwic were withdrawn further inland to Winchester. A new walled settlement was constructed to the west, named Hamtun. In 994 a united force of Vikings under Olaf and Danes under Sweyn arrived in Southampton. It is said that Olaf camped on the eastern bank of the Itchen in an area that became Olaf's Town and later Woolston.

The Saxons paid the Vikings to leave, which they did. However, Sweyn returned many times, demanding monies and sacking the town. The Viking King Canute the Great (r. 1016–35) was Sweyn's son. He defeated the Anglo-Saxon King Ethelred the Unready in 1014. In 1016 Canute met the Witan (Anglo-Saxon parliament) of Saxon England in Southampton and was made King of England. It was also at Southampton that his alleged command to halt the waves is said to have taken place –though this incident was meant to be Canute reproving his courtiers, showing them that even the king was answerable to God.

Southampton has Canute Road, the former Canute Hotel and Canute Chambers – home in 1912 to the White Star Line and where relatives of the *Titanic*'s crew gathered to hear news of their loved ones following its tragic sinking.

Voltaire (1694–1778)

As a young man the French writer and philosopher François-Marie Arouet, better known as Voltaire, was imprisoned in the Bastille, Paris, from 1717 to 1718. Later as an exile in London mixing with English high society, Voltaire was a frequent visitor to Bevois Mount in Southampton. He had been commissioned by estate owner Lord Peterborough to write a substantial work for which he had been given large sums of money in an advance payment from his publisher. One day, the publisher appeared at Bevois Mount and expressed concern to Lord Peterborough. It became clear that Voltaire had spent much of the money and when confronted by Lord Peterborough he took flight. He was in such a hurry to escape Lord Peterborough's wrath that he left behind his portmanteau, papers and other belongings.

W

Warrior

Horses returning from the First World War were sold off. In 1919 actress Hilda Moore contacted the mayor, Sidney Kimber, offering to buy a horse for the town. A large white gelding was handed over to the local police. It had been in France since 1914 and had a battle scar. This warhorse was named Warrior and was popular in the town until its death in 1935. Kimber stepped in and found a grave site for it at the newly opened Municipal Golf Course where it remains with a memorial stone telling Warrior's story.

Watergate

The Watergate was built by 1377, after the French raid of 1338, to strengthen the town's southern defences. In 1403 it was leased to William Revanstone, an ex-mayor, on condition he repaired the tower and gate. His rent was nominal – one red rose payable on 24 June, St John the Baptist day.

Remains of the Watergate at the Town Quay end of the High Street.

Twice mayor and Collector of Customs William Soper (d. 1459) was also Keeper and Governor of the King's Ships. He leased the Watergate on the same conditions. In the part of the tower that still remains there is a four-tier garderobe (toilet). In 1804 the burgesses ordered the gate be pulled down and the stone was sold for 10 shillings. Soper was responsible for the building of the *Grace Dieu* for Henry VII, possibly the biggest ship in the world at that time. She was never used in battle, was laid up in the River Hamble and then caught fire after a lightning strike.

For many years the Sun Hotel was on the site of the east tower. It was rebuilt as the temporary Sun pub by Canadian troops after bombing in 1940 and lasted for many years.

Watts, Isaac (1674–1748)

He was born in Southampton to a nonconformist family. His mother was Sarah Taunton, the daughter of a Huguenot family, and Isaac was the cousin of Richard Taunton, who founded a school in Southampton.

Isaac was seen as such a talented young man that some locals offered to pay his university fees, but nonconformists were not allowed to attend. He was therefore educated at a nonconformist college in Stoke Newington, North London. Despite poor health he embarked on a preaching career in 1698. He also wrote books on logic and poetry but is best remembered today as a prolific hymn writer. He wrote over 500 hymns and 'Our God our Help in Ages Past' is still played from the Civic Centre clock each day. His school was King Edward VI and a house there is still named after him. The statue to him in Watts (West) Park was unveiled on his birthday, 17 July, by the Earl of Shaftesbury in 1861.

Weigh House

The Weigh House was built in French Street in the mid-1200s. The Weigh House once housed a valuable piece of equipment: the town's weigh beam, also known as the Tron. It was used to weigh wool and other goods before sale, so that taxes on these could be accurately calculated. In 1503 Elizabeth Burgess was warden of twelve female woolpackers who worked there. They had a reputation as the 'Wild women of Southampton' and were told 'not to brawl or scold with one another'. During the Second World War it was bombed and only the outer shell remains today.

Welch, Lucia Foster (1864–1940)

Southampton's first female mayor moved to Southampton in 1903 and lived at No. 61 Oxford Street, which is now a Grade II listed building. She was also Southampton's

This portrait of Southampton's first female mayor is outside the Mayor's Parlour in the Civic Centre.

first female Councillor, Sheriff and Alderman. Also in Southampton the Mayor holds the title of Admiral of the Port, so Lucia was England's first Lady Admiral. She was an active member of the Women's Social and Political Union, as well as the National Union of Women's Suffrage Societies.

A portrait in oils of Lucia Foster Welch by Frank Brooks, 1928, can be seen at Southampton Civic Centre outside the Mayor's Parlour.

Windrush Generation

The well-known Windrush arrived in London with 492 passengers in June 1948. There had been previous ships carrying West Indian and Jamaican immigrants. This included the *Almanzora*, which arrived in Southampton with around 200 passengers in December 1947. Some were ex-troops who had fought for Britain in the war. One such, Alan Wilmot, wrote a memoir, *Now You Know*, about the issues he faced in post-war Britain.

The *Almanzora* took part in the First World War, had spent the 1920s and 1930s on the Southampton to River Plate route, was a troopship in the Second World War and was scrapped in 1948.

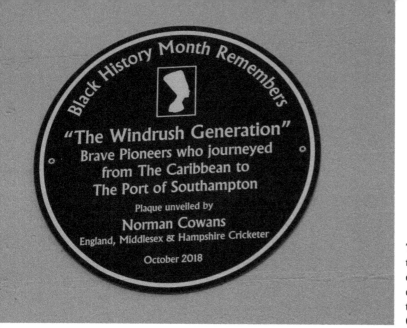

This plaque near the Guildhall side of the Civic Centre commemorates the Windrush Generation.

Women's Football

The first winners of the Women's FA Cup were Southampton WFC in 1971. Southampton-born Sue Lopez played twenty-two games for England and was awarded an MBE in 2000.

Wool House

According to some sources, the late fourteenth-century Wool House was built by the orders of the monks at Beaulieu for use as a secure wool store. It is also said the building and financing of the Wool House was enabled by Thomas Middleton, a wealthy merchant and mayor of Southampton. The Wool House was ideally located right by the quayside so that the wool from all over England could be easily loaded onto the ships.

During the sixteenth century the export of wool and hides declined and finished cloth made by Huguenot weavers became more popular. Eventually the Wool House became a store for alum, which was used as a fixative in dying fabric and in the process of tanning hides.

The Wool House was also used as a prison for captives from the War of the Spanish Succession in the early eighteenth century. The names Francois Dries and Thomas Lasis and the date 1711 still exist. Later French prisoners from the Napoleonic Wars spent their time carving model ships, known as scrimshaws, out of bleached meat bone and making the rigging out of their own hair. Around 1904 it was occupied by the Carron Company, who were manufacturers for warship cannons and also household equipment.

From around 1908 to the mid-1920s, the Wool House was turned into a workshop for a Marine Engineering Company owned by Edwin Moon Snr. His son, Edwin Rowland

Above left: The Dancing Man Brewery makes its own beers on the premises.

Above right: The fourteenth-century former Wool House was once by the quayside.

Below: The Wool House was used as a maritime museum from 1966.

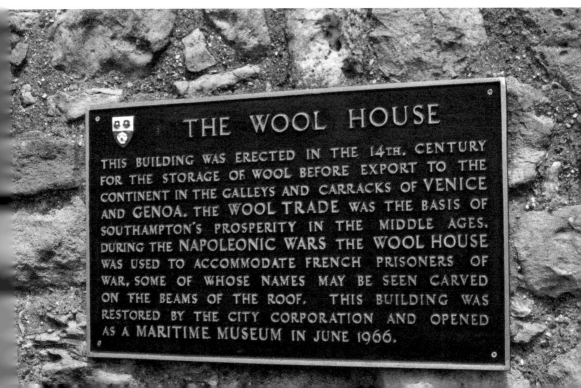

THE WOOL HOUSE

THIS BUILDING WAS ERECTED IN THE 14TH. CENTURY FOR THE STORAGE OF WOOL BEFORE EXPORT TO THE CONTINENT IN THE GALLEYS AND CARRACKS OF VENICE AND GENOA. THE WOOL TRADE WAS THE BASIS OF SOUTHAMPTON'S PROSPERITY IN THE MIDDLE AGES. DURING THE NAPOLEONIC WARS THE WOOL HOUSE WAS USED TO ACCOMMODATE FRENCH PRISONERS OF WAR, SOME OF WHOSE NAMES MAY BE SEEN CARVED ON THE BEAMS OF THE ROOF. THIS BUILDING WAS RESTORED BY THE CITY CORPORATION AND OPENED AS A MARITIME MUSEUM IN JUNE 1966.

Moon, an aviation pioneer who served during the First World War, built his famous monoplane, the *Moonbeam*, in the Wool House. In the early 1960s the building was restored by Southampton Corporation and adapted to house the Maritime Museum, which opened in June 1966 and moved to the new Sea City Museum in 2012.

After extensive renovation this Grade II listed building is now the home of the Dancing Man, which opened as a brewhouse and pub restaurant in 2015.

Workhouse

In 1776 it was decided to build a workhouse to the north of St Mary's churchyard. Despite having the capacity for 220 inmates, it soon became full. It was reported that inmates slept four to a bed and that there was no segregation of the sexes. In 1865 it was decided to build a new workhouse on the land next to the existing one. By 1940 the workhouse was taken over for use as an emergency food centre and following the 1944 Education Act it became the home of Southampton Technical College. Today it houses part of Southampton City College.

World Wide Web

Its founder, Tim Berners Lee (b. 1955), worked at the University of Southampton when the Web was developed in 1989.

Xroads

Southampton is a congested city with many crossroads often used in place of roundabouts. This means control by numerous traffic lights, which many locals feel are rather overused.

X Marks the Spot

Outside Holyrood Church is a brass cross in the pavement. There are two stories connected to this. The first is that it marks the spot where the Catholic Philip II of Spain (1527–98) knelt to thank God that he survived the sea crossing from Spain on his way to marry Queen Mary in Winchester Cathedral in 1554. Another is that on 15 October 1862 the Hartley Institute, the forerunner of the University of Southampton, was opened in the High Street by the Prime Minister Lord Palmerston (1774–1865). Some of crowd climbed onto Holyrood Church to get a better view and dislodged a stone, which crashed down into the crowded street below. Luckily, it did not hit any of the spectators. Following this miracle, the five-time mayor and Liberal MP for Southampton from 1874 to 1880, Sir Fredcrick Perkins (1826–1902) had a brass cross put into the pavement to mark the event. Perhaps the stone landed on the same spot where the king had knelt over 300 years before?

Brass cross in the pavement outside Holy Rood.

Yacht Club

Southampton Yacht Club was formed in 1839 and soon attracted royal patronage. The impressive headquarters at the bottom of Bugle Street next to the former Wool House were built in 1846.

Yevele, Henry (1320–1400)

Both Edward III (1312–77) and Richard II (1367–1400) employed Yevele as Principal Mason and Chief Architect. Between 1378 and 1379 Yevele advised on the building of the new castle keep at Southampton. Southampton Castle was spectacular and rose high above the town. It is thought that Yevele was also the architect for the stretch of walls in Southampton known as 'The Arcades', which were designed to protect the town from attack by the French.

Front view of the Westgate.

Above left: Looking through the medieval walls with St Michael's in the distance.

Above right: Westgate plaque.

Below: The West Quay, *c.* 1450, when it was busy trading with France, Italy and beyond.

Zammit, Joe (1926–2005)

Zammit was Southampton's longest-serving taxi driver for sixty-two years, a spell only broken by service as an army driver in the Second World War. Joe is buried in St Mary's 'Extra Cemetery' in Sholing, Southampton.

This plaque is in the taxi shelter opposite Central station. Joe Zammit was a popular taxi driver with sixty-two years of service.

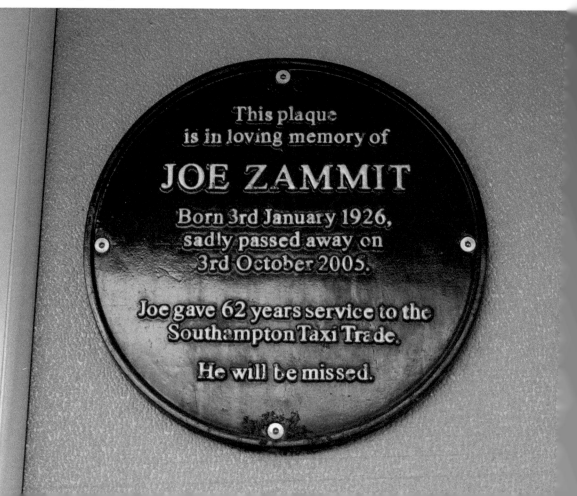

Zip Code

Southampton is covered by the SO14–SO19 postcodes.

Zodiac

The Eastern Docks foundation stone was laid by Admiral Sir Lucius Curtis on 12 October 1838. A column was unveiled just inside No .8 Gate by the Chair of the Southern Railway Company to mark the centenary on 12 October 1938.

At the top was a large bronze globe of the world that has the signs of the zodiac around the equator.

Zoo

Southampton Zoo on the Common was set up by the Chipperfield family in 1961. Some will remember James the smoking chimp. After a successful campaign by animal rights protestors including actors Virginia McKenna and Joanna Lumley the zoo closed in 1985. The site is now the Hawthorns Urban Wildlife Centre and is popular with school groups.

About the Author

As a born and bred Sotonian, I am proud of our city. It has a fascinating heritage and culture that is often overlooked. At present there is considerable inward investment and the city is set for a bright future that is worth letting people know about. Following a career in further and higher education I became a qualified tour guide and founder member of the award-winning See Southampton.

After a brain haemorrhage in 2017 I wrote *Secret Southampton*, followed by this *A–Z of Southampton*. Both have been a valuable part in aiding my recovery. These days I know how fragile life can be and try everyday to value and 'stand and stare' at that which is around me, as summed up in *Leisure* by W. H. Davies (1911):

> What is this life if, full of care,
> We have no time to stand and stare.
> No time to stand beneath the boughs
> And stare as long as sheep or cows.
> No time to see, when woods we pass,
> Where squirrels hide their nuts in grass.
> No time to see, in broad daylight,
> Streams full of stars, like skies at night.
> No time to turn at Beauty's glance,
> And watch her feet, how they can dance.
> No time to wait till her mouth can
> Enrich that smile her eyes began.
> A poor life this if, full of care,
> We have no time to stand and stare.